SM. 9900 3928
JIC X
1/08
(Can)
13.99

SCHOOLS IN CYBERSPACE

A PRACTICAL GUIDE TO USING THE INTERNET IN SCHOOLS

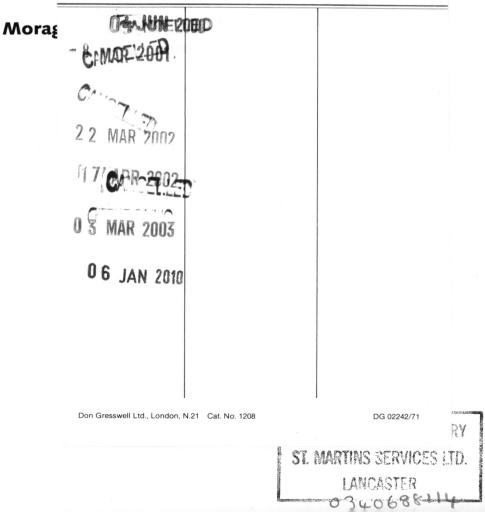

Orders: please contact Bookpoint Ltd, 78 Milton Park, Abingdon, Oxon OX14 4TD. Telephone: (44) 01235 400454. Lines are open from 9.00 - 6.00, Monday to Saturday, with a 24 hour message answering service. Email address: orders@bookpoint.co.uk

British Library Cataloguing in Publication Data
A catalogue entry for this title is available from the British Library

ISBN 0 340 68811 4

First published 1997
Impression number   10 9 8 7 6 5 4 3 2
Year   2005 2004 2003 2002 2001 2000 1999

Typeset by Wearset, Boldon, Tyne and Wear.
Printed in Great Britain for Hodder & Stoughton Educational, a division of Hodder Headline Plc, 338 Euston Road, London NW1 3BH by Scotprint Ltd, Musselburgh, Scotland.

Contents

Acknowledgements

The authors would like to acknowledge the support of the University of Strathclyde, and in particular the Department of Business and Computer Education, in providing us with the resources we needed to develop our own expertise and try out the ideas described in this book.

We would also like to thank the staff and pupils of St Helen's Primary School, Condorrat, Cumbernauld for their help in developing some of the practical examples.

Morag, Fionna and David would like to thank Jim, Gordon and Janet for all their encouragement, help and support.

The book is dedicated to Morag's sons, Stephen and Brian, Fionna's daughters, Gail, Laura and Sally and David's daughters, Rachel, Rebekah and Sarah.

Disclaimer

Every effort was made to ensure that the Internet

resources given in this book were correct at the time of going to press. However, items on the Internet are constantly being updated and some links become invalid. The authors have created a set of World Wide Web pages to accompany this book which will be reviewed on a regular basis to ensure that sets of relevant links are always available.

Chapter 1

Let's start at the very beginning

Age range

This book describes work suitable for primary school children aged 10 to 12. However many of the ideas could be adapted and used with younger pupils. For example a teacher could summarise the information and present it in a manner more appropriate to his or her children, rather than allowing them to access the material directly from the Internet.

The book could also be used with older pupils who may be able to access a greater range of sites and carry out further research on their own. Some sites contain useful information, but the reading level required make them more suitable for children in this age range.

How this book works

The authors hope that this book will inspire confidence

in and enthusiasm for the use of the Internet in the classroom. Chapters 2 to 4 deal with general information about the Internet. We hope that you find them interesting and informative and more importantly non-threatening!

Chapters 5 to 9 contain curricular examples – sets of suggestions describing how use of the Internet could be incorporated into a number of classroom topics. They are intended to be a stimulus and a guide to your work in the classroom. The examples are not prescriptive, so a teacher could take some ideas from Chapter 8 (the newspaper chapter) but use it in a different context. The newspaper project could be combined with ideas from Chapter 5 (Sports in Cyberspace) to produce newspaper reports on the sporting events carried out by schools throughout the world.

There are many factors which govern the use of the Internet in schools and within these chapters alternative ways of using the Internet resources are addressed.

At the end of the curricular chapters there are lists of useful Internet sites relevant to the subject. The lists are only starting points and no doubt you will find other useful and relevant sites.

Glossary entries

Computing is notorious for its use of impenetrable jargon, making it difficult for the uninitiated to understand even simple concepts. To try and guide you through this jungle of jargon we have provided a Glossary, a Cyberspeak Translator.

The first time a new term is used in the book it will be highlighted in bold and a definition for this term will be found in the Glossary, which also contains definitions of some other terms in common use. In particular many of the commonly used acronyms are expanded and explained.

Worksheets

Chapters 5 to 9 have accompanying worksheets to support the topics described. These worksheets can be copied by private purchasers for their own use or for use by their own students; school purchasers may make copies for use within and by the staff and students of the school.

These worksheets could be used as extension work or simply to give the teacher ideas on how the topic could be developed and integrated with other work carried out in the classroom.

On-line support for the book

To help keep you up to date support for this book is also available on the Internet. The location of this site, and details on how to access it, can be found in Chapter 2. This site will not only keep you up-to-date about relevant resources, but will also make them easier to access. They will be available at the click of a button rather than having to type complicated instructions copied from this book.

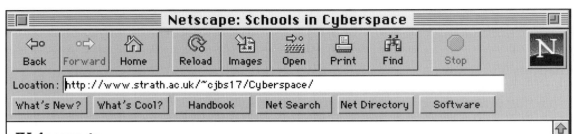

Netscape: Schools in Cyberspace

⇐o Back	o⇒ Forward	🏠 Home	ℝ Reload	🖼 Images	⇒° Open	🖨 Print	🔍 Find	○ Stop	**N**

Location : http://www.strath.ac.uk/~cjbs17/Cyberspace/

What's New?	What's Cool?	Handbook	Net Search	Net Directory	Software

Welcome to...

 # Schools in Cyberspace
A practical guide for schools on the Internet

Schools in Cyberspace

This is a collection of pages with links, hints and tips to help you get the most of the Internet as a resource to support learning and teaching.

We hope you enjoy these resources. Please send us any comments you may have about what we have included or omitted. We're looking forward to hearing from you!

Exploring Cyberspace

The order of the sections listed below matches the chapter order of the book *Schools in Cyberspace: A practical guide to using the Internet in schools*, published by Hodder and Stoughton.

- Let's Start At the Very Beginning.

- Lost in Cyberspace.

Chapter 2
Lost in Cyberspace

Introduction

It is difficult to escape the hype surrounding the **Internet**. Newspapers, magazines, television, films . . . every type of media seems to be featuring the Internet – even the Tetley Tea man and Action Man have Internet addresses! Barbie has an on-line description of her CD-Rom Software.

Some claims for the Internet seem excessively over enthusiastic. For example, that the global communication made possible by the Internet will usher in a new era of world peace and co-operation, or that it is the next step in human evolution. Others have suggested that once schools are properly equipped with Internet access, they will be able to do without teachers and that school buildings could become redundant as children are educated at home. Such statements do little to help convince teachers of the potential of the Internet as a serious and useful educational tool. For the foreseeable future the Internet is as likely to make teachers redundant as the video cassette recorder.

This book gives examples of practical activities which can be carried out with the Internet. The reader can decide how useful or essential a tool the Internet is for each activity. By giving practical examples, it is hoped to avoid the more extravagant claims which contaminate many sources of information about the Internet. However it may be that on occasions the authors' enthusiasm for their subject will get the better of them. Always remember to look critically at the ideas presented and decide how relevant they are to your unique situation and needs.

What is the Internet?

Many books which seek to introduce the Internet start with a potted history: who invented it; who runs it; how it works. While they may be interesting and possibly even useful, it is out of place in a practical guide such as this. Any of the general guides will tell you what you want to know. Instead this chapter will explain some of the ways in which the Internet can be used to support learning and teaching, and will introduce the skills and conventions that will help you use it more effectively.

An accurate but not particularly helpful description of the Internet is that it is a network of networks. A **network** is simply a group of computers which are linked together so that they can share information. This means that when you attach a computer to the Internet, it is possible to access information held on millions of computers spread around the world.

With such a technical description, it is difficult to see why so many people are getting excited about the Internet. Being able to connect a computer to millions of others does not sound like the sort of activity which will excite, involve and educate children in our schools.

One aspect which makes it more interesting is the people who use the computers connected to the

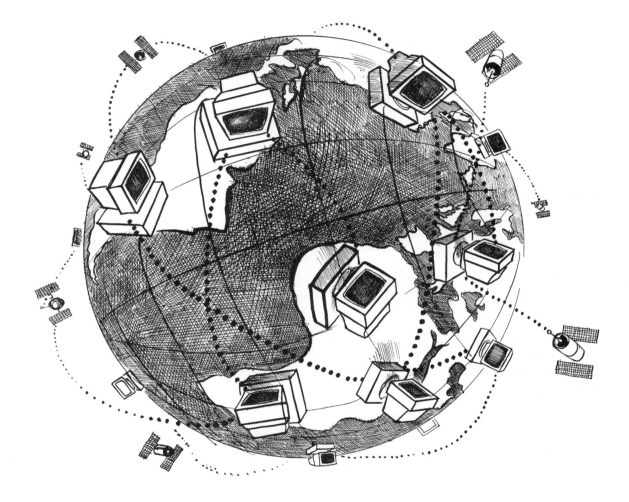

Internet. It is difficult to get exact figures, but at the
time of writing there is estimated to be around 35
million people who can **surf** the Internet. It is also
difficult to obtain precise demographics for the people
who use the Internet, but most studies suggest a large
percentage of users are based in colleges and
universities in North America. However the range of
people connected is increasing all the time. In particular
many schools across the world, teaching children of all
ages, are joining the Internet.

Since there is such a vast number of people connected,
you are almost certain to find someone with a common

"On the Internet, nobody knows you're a dog."

interest, someone to co-operate with, or someone who will help when you encounter difficulties. It can be surprising just how much help you can get from people on the Internet and how willing they are to spend time helping you.

For example a researcher in a university received a question sent by **electronic mail**. An answer was sent off more or less straight away but the researcher did not realise that the question had come from school pupils. The pupils asked if a simpler explanation was possible and one was soon sent off by the researcher. Can you imagine what would happen if a pupil wrote a letter asking for information for a school project? Yet the researcher was willing to take the time to answer a question from a complete stranger. On the Internet nobody knows you're a school pupil! Other users of the Internet need only know as much or as little about you as you choose to reveal.

Where do I start?

One way to start is to consider what tools are available to help you use the Internet. This section will highlight two Internet applications, namely electronic mail and the **World Wide Web**.

Electronic mail (e-mail)

Electronic mail was mentioned above as the way the school pupils asked the researcher the question, but what is it and how does it work? Electronic mail is very simple in concept. Essentially it is a way of sending messages, often simple text messages, from one computer to another without printing the message on paper or sending discs between computers.

What then are the advantages of using electronic mail? Firstly there is the often quoted speed advantage. It is possible to send a message to someone on the other side of the world and receive a reply before a letter has even been collected from the post-box. Also, you are free from worry about time zones. Is Australia ahead or

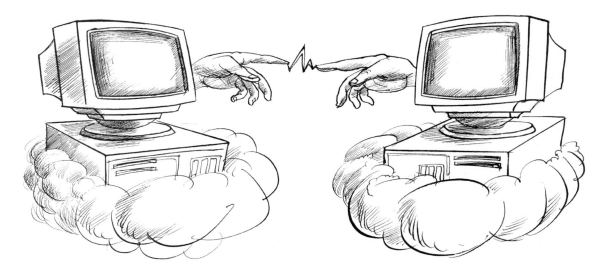

behind us in time? Will the person be at work or in bed? Electronic mail cuts through all of these problems because when you send a message it is stored electronically until the recipient chooses to read it.

These are general advantages of electronic mail, but what about its advantages for schools? One major advantage is that pupils can use word processing to create messages, then polish and check until they are satisfied with the result before using electronic mail to send it to the intended recipient. If necessary the messages can be checked by a teacher or by peers. This can lead to greater confidence as most pupils (in fact most people) feel happier sending a carefully thought out message to a stranger than they would phoning the same person and asking for the information. A second advantage is that messages can be sent to the other side of the world for the same cost as sending a message to someone who lives down the road. This opens up the possibility of affordable and accessible communication with people from other cultures and other countries.

It is because we have a unique postal address that we are able to receive letters and parcels. In the same way, in order for electronic mail to work there must be a way to uniquely identify each machine and individual on the Internet. This unique identifier is known as an electronic mail address.

World Wide Web

The World Wide Web is another Internet application. When the Internet is featured in the media, it is almost always the World Wide Web which is shown. In fact some people assume that the World Wide Web *is* the Internet, which it is not. It is however an increasingly popular Internet application.

The World Wide Web was designed in Europe at the European Particle Physics Laboratory (known as CERN) to support communication among members of the high

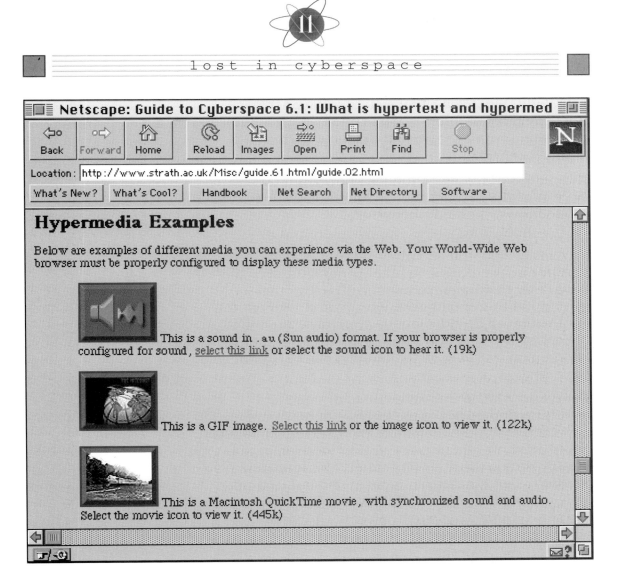

energy-physics community. From relatively humble beginnings, the World Wide Web concept has grown and now allows the transmission and display of a wide variety of information – pictures, video, animation, sound – as well as text which can be displayed in different sizes, styles and colours. The variety of objects which can be displayed may make the information look more attractive and the dynamic nature of some of these objects (for example sound and animation) make for a much richer information source than text alone. This is especially important for the 'post Nintendo generation' which is used to a multiplicity of information sources.

The World Wide Web allows you to move on screen from one piece of information to another, often simply by pointing with a mouse and clicking a button. This facility is known as **hypertext**.

This process of following **links** is known as browsing, or more informally as surfing. The software which enables you to browse is called a **browser**.

A page of information from the World Wide Web could have many links, some to other sections of the page already displayed, some to other pages written by the same author and some to pages written by other people. It is this web of links, which can stretch out to information all over the world, which gives the World Wide Web its name. It is possible to access much of the information available on the Internet just by following these links.

The World Wide Web is an exciting, dynamic and rapidly expanding use of the Internet (it has been estimated that more than three thousand new pages of information are added every week). However, at the time of writing the greatest amount of information transferred on the Internet is generated by electronic mail. Although the World Wide Web is flashy and exciting, for many people the essential Internet application remains electronic mail.

The main problem with the World Wide Web is that just about anybody can use it to publish their own information. This can cause problems since some of the information will be inaccurate or misleading. Some of it will obviously be rubbish, and although there will be other pages which may look authoritative, often they are not. One indicator of the validity of the information is its source (the next section explains how to work this out).

Another problem is that the information is not always designed to be read by children. Many useful resources will have to be filtered through a teacher or another adult before they could be used by children. Methods of preventing access to unsuitable material are discussed on pages 25–28.

What's out there?

It is all very well knowing that there are over 35 million people with electronic mail and three thousand new World Wide Web pages every week, but how do you find out the electronic mail addresses of people you would like to contact, or the location of a particular page of information? A question many people ask is whether there is the electronic mail equivalent of a telephone directory. Although attempts are made to create directories, the rapidly changing nature of the Internet makes them outdated almost as soon as they become available. Currently the easiest way to find someone's electronic mail address is to ask them. (For example friends of one of the authors, who are currently staying in Peru, had just acquired electronic mail. After a frustrating evening failing to discover the author's electronic mail address, they had to admit defeat and ask for it by writing a letter!)

---

f.h.kent@strath.ac.uk, How goes the work?

| BIN HEX | ✓ QP | 🗐 | ✓ 🖼 | ✓ ↠ | ✓ 🗖 | ✓ ⌘ | Send |

```
        To: f.h.kent@strath.ac.uk
      From: d.d.muir@strath.ac.uk (David Muir)
   Subject: How goes the work?
        Cc:
       Bcc:
Attachments:
```

```
Hi Fionna,

How goes the work on the book? I'm getting seriously scunnered with it, but
hopefully you are getting on better.

David
```

How to read addresses

An electronic mail address is similar to a postal address which normally contains a person's name to uniquely identify the recipient, followed by the house number, street name, town and possibly country to uniquely identify his or her location. An electronic mail address contains similar elements. By way of an example, the electronic mail address of one of the authors is explained below.

d.d.muir@strath.ac.uk

First the section up to the @ sign identifies the person, in this case David Muir. There are two Ds because David has a middle name (Dalrymple in case anyone is interested). The use of middle names can help create unique identifiers, for example helping distinguish David from Donald Muir, without making the address too unwieldy.

The section after the @ sign (pronounced 'at') identifies David's location. In this case it shows that his mail is stored on a computer at Strathclyde University ('strath'), which is an academic institution ('ac') in the United Kingdom ('uk').

If you were telling somebody this address, perhaps on the telephone, you would normally pronounce the '.' as 'dot' rather than 'period' or 'full stop', so the whole address would be pronounced:

D dot D dot Muir at strath dot ac dot uk.

Most electronic mail addresses end in a two letter code which identifies a country – 'uk' for the United Kingdom, 'de' for Germany, 'au' for Australia and so on. The exception to this is the United States of America. In the same way that the United Kingdom does not put its name on stamps (because we thought of them first!) so the USA does not always identify itself in electronic addresses. Although some more recently assigned addresses will use a 'us' code, most use a three letter code to identify the type of organisation which

holds the addressee's mail. For example 'edu' for an education establishment, 'gov' for a government organisation and 'com' for a commercial company. An example of such an address is:

president@whitehouse.gov

Note that these two example addresses really work. If you have access to an electronic mail system, try sending a short message to each and see what happens.

```
┌─────────────────────────────────────────────────────┐
│ ▣  ▦▦▦▦▦  president@whitehouse.gov, Hello  ▦▦▦▦  ▣  │
├─────────────────────────────────────────────────────┤
│ ┌──┐ BIN  ✓ QP    ▣    ✓⊞   ✓⊣   ✓▢   ✓⌘  ( Send ) │
│ └──┘ HEX                                              │
├─────────────────────────────────────────────────────┤
│           To: president@whitehouse.gov          ⬆    │
│         From: m.f.cunningham@strath.ac.uk (Morag ▦   │
│      Subject: Hello                    Cunningham)   │
│           Cc:                                         │
│          Bcc:                                         │
│  Attachments:                                         │
│  ···················································   │
│  Hello Mr Clinton                                    │
│                                                       │
│  Just wondered how Socks the cat was getting on.     │
│                                                       │
│  All the best.                                       │
│                                                       │
│  Morag.                                        ⬇    │
│                                               ▣     │
└─────────────────────────────────────────────────────┘
```

How to access the World Wide Web

In the same way that every person with access to electronic mail must have an address, so each piece of information on the World Wide Web must be uniquely identified so that it can be accessed directly rather than by browsing through hypertext links. The unique identifier is known as a **Uniform Resource Locator**.

Diversion

       The term Uniform Resource Locator is often shortened to **URL**. This is the first example in this book of the alphabet soup of acronyms which plague users of the Internet. Stephen Hawking in his introduction to *A Brief History of Time* says he was told that each equation he included in the book would halve the sales. The authors have the feeling that the same could be true of this book and the use of acronyms, therefore the full expansion of terms (such as Uniform Resource Locator) will be used throughout this book. However, since the abbreviated forms are in such common use, some of the more common acronyms are included in a Glossary at the end of the book.

This book has a page on the Internet!

A source of information to accompany this book has been created and is available through the World Wide Web. The Uniform Resource Locator which allows access to this information is:

http://www.strath.ac.uk/~cjbs17/Cyberspace/index.html

Uniform Resource Locators explained

Although it may be helpful to explain some of the apparently meaningless collections of letters which make up a Uniform Resource Locator you do not really have to understand them to use them. However, a brief explanation is provided below. Do not panic if, even after reading the explanation, it still looks like Greek!

The first section of the Uniform Resource Locator is yet another acronym! The '**http**' is an access method identifier, in other words it shows what type of

information is accessed by this locator. In this case, 'http' stands for **hypertext transport protocol** and all it means is that the information which will be accessed is a World Wide Web hypertext page.

The next section 'www.strath.ac.uk' looks similar to the electronic mail address given earlier and performs the same function – it identifies the location of the machine which stores the information.

The remaining sections further refine the location of the information, defining exactly where the information is held until the final part, 'index.html' which identifies the document to be retrieved.

All browsers have a way of entering Uniform Resource Locators so that you can jump directly to some piece of information. There are shelves of books and magazines which list hundreds of Uniform Resource Locators. Many advertisements and television programmes now direct you to a Web site where further information is displayed. To make use of these, all you have to do is carefully type the Uniform Resource Locator into the browser program.

Schools in Cyberspace Web Pages

As sites change and disappear, so do *Uniform Resource Locators*, so a collection of World Wide Web pages has been created to accompany this book. This site will try to keep the links current and if any of the locations suggested in the book disappear, the Schools in **Cyberspace** Web pages will try to suggest alternatives. All the information sources described in this book are displayed as hypertext links on the Schools in Cyberspace page, which will save you some typing. The Uniform Resource Locator for this page is in fact the one given in the example earlier, namely:

http://www.strath.ac.uk/~cjbs17/Cyberspace/index.html

Where can I find out more?

Some of the issues introduced in this section are dealt with more fully on the World Wide Web itself. A few places to start looking are listed below (and on the Schools in Cyberspace Web pages).

The Online Netskills Interactive Course

http://www.netskills.ac.uk/TONIC/

The Online Netskills Interactive Course (TONIC) is a good introduction to the Internet. It offers step-by-step practical guidance on major Internet topics, ranging from the basic through to the advanced.

The Net: User Guidelines and Netiquette

http://www.fau.edu/rinaldi/netiquette.html

This set of pages indicated above deals with the area of Internet use which is (unfortunately) known as 'netiquette'. The Internet can seem a baffling place at first. If you want to avoid the more obvious mistakes, Arlene Rinaldi's on-line guide is a readable introduction to this particular minefield.

. . . and finally!

Just in case you are interested, Action Man's Web address is:

http://www.actionman.com/

Barbie's on-line guide to her CD-Roms can be found at:

http://www.mattelmedia.com/barbie/index.html

and the Tetley Tea man's electronic mail address is:

gaffer@tetley.co.uk

Chapter 3
First steps in Cyberspace

How can I use it?

After the general introduction to the Internet in Chapter 2, it is time to look more closely at its educational uses. The Internet can be used in the classroom in a variety of ways, but is best seen as a means to an end rather than an end in itself. The examples given in subsequent chapters should always be checked against the curricular aims you have set for your class, to see which uses would best match its needs. Often these needs will be best met with resources other than the Internet. This section and the examples given later should help you to identify areas of the curriculum and types of activity which will benefit most from access to the Internet. Three main categories of use are described below.

❶ Electronic version of existing practice

There are many classroom activities which have an Internet counterpart. An obvious example is electronic penpals. (Some people have started calling them keypals.) It is not uncommon for schools to encourage pupils to have penpals, to aid the development of writing skills and an awareness of other cultures. The use of electronic mail does not significantly change the activity, but it does bring speed advantages which can help maintain interest.

Seeking information from other people is another typical activity. Swapping information, asking questions and offering support can take place in a variety of ways: teacher to teacher; pupil to pupil; teacher to pupil; teacher to expert; expert to pupil.

Again the Internet can help facilitate this kind of communication, perhaps extending the scope of the people that can be approached. For example the 'expert' may be a personal contact known to the teacher or pupil. It may be a person who has made it known that he or she is willing to answer questions. It could have been set up through an organised 'ask an expert' scheme. The expert could be:

- a real life adventurer sending e-mail from an expedition as it is happening;
- a fictitious character such as the captain of a spaceship travelling to a strange new world;
- even someone pretending to be a figure from history such as Henry VIII.

Some organisations actively seek to serve education by setting up such contacts. See for example the Internet For Learning's projects page:

http://www.rmplc.co.uk/meeting/proj.html

As well as person to person contact, it is possible to contact groups of people through mailing lists or list servers. There are lists to cater for many different interests. From a school's point of view they are a useful way of contacting a large number of people interested in a common topic. A useful list of educational resources, including mailing lists (follow the 'Listserv' link), can be found at:

http://k12.cnidr.org:90/k12.html

❷   Adding a new dimension to existing practice

Other common classroom activities can be enhanced by access to the Internet. It could provide a global audience or test bed for work normally carried out in the classroom or give up-to-date information in an easily accessible form.

One example is a simple survey of television viewing habits. Perhaps a class could keep a diary of their television viewing for a week. Typical classroom activities based around this would include working out averages, comparing boys' habits with girls' and drawing graphs to illustrate the results. By contacting other schools around the country, or even in different countries, other possibilities arise. For example comparing the results of rural areas with urban or the results from different countries. The ease of collecting and disseminating such work on the Internet allows the

teacher to add this extra dimension with little extra effort.

Another example is a newspaper survey. (An example of this use is given in Chapter 8.) Teachers may encourage pupils to look at the ways different newspapers report the same story. Since many newspapers now publish World Wide Web editions, it would be possible to look at how different countries report the same news. The Internet adds a global dimension to this common activity. Also there will be a sense of accessing the news 'as it happens', adding to the excitement of the activity.

❸ Going beyond existing practice

There are some activities which the Internet can support which it would be difficult to carry through by other means. The use of the Internet in schools is still at an early stage of development, especially in the United Kingdom, but as teachers become more familiar with the Internet and explore its possibilities, the number of new activities are likely to increase.

One organisation which is putting a great deal of information on the Internet, some of it specifically aimed at schools, is the National Aeronautics and Space Administration (NASA). Images from the Hubble Space Telescope, details of Shuttle missions, activities involving pupils in space related experiments are placed on the World Wide Web by NASA. Some of the activities could be carried out without the Internet, but the live nature of the information creates an atmosphere and excitement that is difficult to match. Children can be reading text describing findings and viewing images from NASA at the same time as it is made available to scientists around the world. An example of this were the images of the Shoemaker-Levy 9 comet striking Jupiter in July 1994, which were placed on the Internet as they came into NASA from the Hubble Telescope. Some of the images are still available at:

http://seds.lpl.arizona.edu/sl9/sl9.html

NASA is a very good source of information and projects. Space as a topic of study is dealt with more thoroughly in Chapter 9.

Another example of a new use is a project initiated by a teacher in North America. The teacher had been talking about the phases of the moon with the class. One of the pupils asked if when there was a full moon where they lived, would people in other parts of the world see a full moon too? The teacher admitted that she did not know. It would be possible to check almanacs or text books, but she wished to involve the pupils in a more practical exercise. As a result it was decided to ask schools around the world to note the phase of the moon on a particular date and send the information back to her class by electronic mail. This allowed the pupils to discover the answer for themselves, making it more real than if the teacher had simply looked up the answer and told them.

Chapter 4
Exploring in Cyberspace

Law and responsibility

In Chapter 2 we talked about the hype that currently surrounds the Internet, but for every story in the media praising the Internet there is another which reveals a part of its darker side ('. . . and with just a couple of clicks our children could be accessing plans on how to make a bomb').

Although it could be argued that this type of material is equally accessible in public libraries, there is no denying that there is material available on the Internet which it would not be appropriate to access in schools. How do schools cope with this? Is it possible to prevent children from viewing undesirable material?

It is possible to block much of the undesirable aspects of the Internet. This can be achieved by choosing an **Internet Service Provider** who undertakes responsibility for blocking access to certain areas. Or it is possible to buy a program such as *SurfWatch*™ or *Net Nanny*™ which can be set to screen out certain areas of the Internet.

governments around the world become more aware of the Internet and as businesses wish to make use of it for commercial purposes, information providers will come under increasing pressure to act responsibly and within the law. Already a system of rating pages, similar to the certification system applied to films, has been implemented. Browser programs can be set to prevent access to pages which have a particular rating and to block information which carries no rating. Currently this rating scheme is voluntary, and it is not clear how widely it will be adopted. However Microsoft has thrown its not inconsiderable weight behind the scheme, so there is a strong possibility that it will become a standard method of restricting access. The scheme is known as the Platform for Internet Content Selection (PICS) and information on how it works can be found at:

http://www.w3.org/pub/WWW/PICS/

However, no system is infallible and schools should be wary of relying on such schemes and programs. Schools should, at the very least, take steps to prepare children to use the Internet responsibly. They should also teach children what to do if they do come across inappropriate material. It has already been said that 'On the Internet, nobody knows you're a dog', but the problem is that nobody knows if you are a wolf in sheep's clothing either. It is possible to build up a relationship with someone by electronic mail, apparently becoming friends, but children should be warned that if they ever meet 'electronic mail friends' they should treat them as they would treat a stranger.

Acceptable Use Policy

This concern about possible misuse of the Internet has led many schools to create what has become known as an **Acceptable Use Policy**. Typically this defines the educational uses and benefits of the Internet. It also states the responsibilities of pupils, parents and teachers, as well as the penalties for inappropriate uses. The process of creating such a policy document can be valuable in itself by making staff aware of the pitfalls and the simple, practical steps which can be taken to minimise the dangers. Some schools invite parents to the school for a demonstration of the potential of the Internet and the safeguards the school has adopted. Further discussion of acceptable use policies, as well as examples, can be found at:

http://chico.rice.edu/armadillo/acceptable.html

An example of the type of problem which such steps may fail to prevent is detailed in *The Ballad of an Email Terrorist* by Al Rogers, whose Uniform Resource Locator is shown on page 28. This article details the chain of events which were started when a young pupil received an offensive electronic mail message.

Despite what was said in the previous chapter about the anonymity of the Internet, it is usually possible to

track the originator of offensive material. The article describes this tracking process, what happened to the originator of the message and includes suggestions on how to prepare children (and teachers) to deal with similar problems should they arise. The article can be accessed at:

http://www.gsn.org/gsn/articles/article.email.ballad.html

Frequently Asked Questions

When seeking the answer to a problem you will often find that others have already encountered it too. If others have asked for the same help, there is a good chance that the question and answer have been recorded. Therefore, when seeking help on any given topic, it is often a good idea to look for a **Frequently Asked Questions** list first and see if someone has already solved your problem. Frequently Asked Questions is often abbreviated to **FAQ**. The term is a bit of a misnomer and the set of information would be better named as Answers to Frequently Asked Questions. The main purpose of these documents is to provide answers to commonly asked questions on a given topic. An example of such a document, which answers questions on the WWWEdu mailing list such as what is 'WWWEdu' and 'how do I subscribe to it', can be found at:

http://k12.cnidr.org:90/wwwedu.faq.html

Searching for information

Although the 'truth is out there!', finding it can sometimes feel like a job for the FBI. It is estimated that there are thousands of sources of information accessible on the World Wide Web. New pages are being added every day as well as old pages disappearing, moving or losing relevance. This makes it impossible for people to keep an accurate check on all sources available. Ironically one of the benefits of the Internet (the availability of large quantities of up-to-date information) can also be the cause of a major problem (finding the needle of relevant information in the disorganised haystack of available data). Therefore to find information you often have to rely on computer assistance.

Search engines

There are a number of programs which search the Internet for you and catalogue what they find. These programs are known as **search engines**. It is usually possible to type in a few keywords which the search engine will check against the keywords in its catalogue. It will then display links to all the sites which match the given keywords.

Two examples of search engines are:

http://www.yahoo.co.uk/

and

http://www.webcrawler.com/

The difficulty is that a keyword search can produce thousands of matches. It can take a considerable amount of time to work through even a fraction of the links suggested, many of which could prove redundant or contain information related to the keywords, but not specifically relevant to your enquiry. One of the authors discovered an example of this while helping pupils to search for information on their favourite pop groups. One girl was looking for information on the band *Wet Wet Wet*. When this was entered into the search engine, the link which appeared at the top of the results list directed the pupil to information on bed-wetting!

Some search engines organise their links into subject categories so that you can narrow down your search by following a series of links which take you progressively nearer your goal. This can often be very effective as, when you find one site containing the type of information you are interested in, it will almost certainly contain links to similar resources elsewhere.

If you use a search engine regularly, it is worth spending some time learning how best to use its facilities. There is almost always a help or hints section which explains how to get the best results. Each search engine uses a slightly different way of specifying the search. For example, say you wanted to search for information on schools television programmes. Obvious keywords to try are 'television', 'schools' and 'education'. What you want are sites which have information related to both television and schools, or television and education. With some search engines, typing in all three words will find pages that mention any one of the keywords, others will only find pages which contain references to all three. Usually you can force the search engine to find the correct combination but you may have to spend some time reading the help pages to find out how.

Remembering where you have been

The very nature of the World Wide Web encourages users to wander through the available information. It is possible to start off looking for one piece of information, but to be side-tracked into a completely different line of enquiry by an interesting link. It is all too easy to end up at a useful source of information without having any clear idea how you got there, or any guarantee about being able to remember how to return at some time in the future.

To help overcome this difficulty, browser programs normally provide a facility for recording the location of a site so that you can return to it easily whenever you choose. Many browsers, including *Netscape Navigator*™

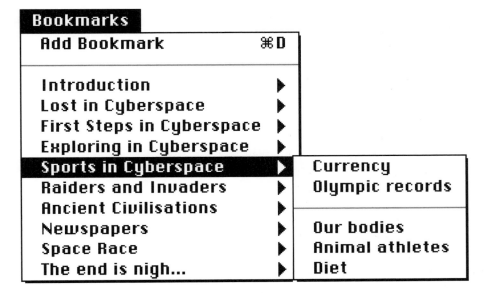

call this list of locations a **bookmark** list, and to record a location you would add a bookmark. (Microsoft calls this a **'Favourites'** list in the *Internet Explorer*™ browser.)

It is often possible to structure bookmarks by subdividing the locations into different categories. This can be very useful in schools where a teacher could do the hard work of finding and cataloguing a set of useful locations related to a topic. The teacher can then create the bookmarks and structure them to make the sites easily accessible for the pupils studying the topic.

Putting information on the World Wide Web

Chapter 2 described the World Wide Web and showed how rapidly it is growing. One of the reasons for this rapid growth is that it is relatively easy to add information – anyone can become a Web publisher. The information which is sent to browsers is essentially text. It is the responsibility of the browser program to interpret that text file and display the Web page to the user.

You can design very complex pages with the simplest of word processors, however it can all look rather daunting. Thankfully there are a number of aids to creating pages available. For example many word processors have the ability to save in **html** format (for example *Claris Works*™ and *Microsoft Word*™). Other programs have been written specifically to create Web pages (for example *Aldus PageMill*™ and *Claris Home Page*™). These tools, and others like them, are making it increasingly simple to create and publish World Wide Web pages.

Although it is possible to make Web pages accessible to the whole world, it is just as possible to use them to display local information. Browsers can access pages stored on your own disk as well as pages stored on the World Wide Web. This allows schools to create their own Web pages and try them out on a single machine, or on all the machines in one room. Pupils could create simple multimedia resources and display them on machines in the school on parents' nights or open days.

HTML in the raw! (not for the faint-hearted)

The text files describing the Web pages use a language known as **HyperText Markup Language (HTML)**. This language describes the format of the page using markup tags. These tags are always enclosed in angle brackets (< and >) and usually come in pairs, for example:

<B>This text should be displayed in bold</B>

An example of a simple Web page is shown below:

<HTML>
<HEAD>
<TITLE>Simple Web Page</TITLE>
</HEAD>

<BODY>
Hello world! Here is my <B>first</B> page designed for the <I>World Wide Web</I>.

</BODY>
</HTML>

Every Web page should start with **<HTML>** and end with **</HTML>**. This page is then split into two sections. First the **<HEAD>** section, which normally contains the **<TITLE>** of the page (i.e. the text displayed in the title bar). This is followed by the **<BODY>** section (usually the largest) containing the text, hypertext and links to graphics.

If you wish you can type in the example page, shown above, into a word processor. When you save the file, make sure you save it as plain text, not in the word processor's native format. Also you should add .html at the end of the file's name (for example, Test.html).

Start your browser program and open the text file you have just created. (Most browsers allow you to open files stored on your own machines disk as well as using Uniform Resource Locators to access information stored elsewhere). Check how the page is displayed. It is not particularly exciting!

Chapter 5
Sports in Cyberspace

Introduction

International sporting events generate a great deal of interest among the young and have for many years been a rich context around which to develop a cross-curricular topic with your pupils.

The Internet enables a new dimension to be added. When the Olympics, Commonwealth Games, European Games, or any large event is taking place many schools take the opportunity to run mini events with their own pupils; the Internet allows your pupils to take part in international competition without ever leaving the school grounds!

This sports example highlights the dynamic dimension of the Internet. Not only is it used as an up-to-the-minute source of information but also allows the pupils to co-operate, collaborate, communicate and compete with pupils around the world.

The Topic Web on page 43 illustrates the way in which a class developed a topic around the theme of the

Olympic Games. Obviously similar topics would be
suitable to coincide with other major events and we
hope that this example will highlight the Internet's
potential and give you the enthusiasm and confidence
to develop your own sporting topic.

Case Study

A class in a city school of 11–12-year-olds were excited
by the build up to the Olympic Games and their teacher
harnessed this enthusiasm and used it as a foundation
on which to build the work of the class for that term.

The main focus of the topic was on English Language,
Maths, Science and PE, although as can be seen from
the topic web on page 43 most areas of the curriculum
were addressed. The children had access to the Internet
which enabled this topic to become an interactive,
exciting subject for learning.

Calling all participants

Through the Internet the children contacted other schools around the world and invited them to take part in a Schools Cyberspace Olympics.

The first stage of their journey into Cyberspace was to make contact with other schools which might be interested in entering the Games the pupils hoped to host. This was done through a variety of **Newsgroups** and user groups.

Spanish Schools:
http://www.worldwide.edu/ci/spain/index.html

French Schools:
http://www.worldwide.edu/ci/france/index.html

Hong Kong Schools:
http://www.worldwide.edu/index.html

Newsgroups:
news:k12.chat.teacher

The pupils also set up a **Home Page** to have a meeting place for all those involved in their Games and this allowed every school to have access to any data collected. It was decided to limit the number of schools involved in their Games to ten, while covering as many countries as possible. Greater number would have made management of the project more difficult. Once contact had been established with enough interested schools the teacher offered to share the plan of the project with any other school wanting to set up their own Games.

Rules and regulations

Through communication with the other schools the format of the Games was established; suitable events were identified and rules established (for example regarding age range). It was decided that not only would there be individual winners for events, but also that the average for each school team in an event would be taken as the team score and that medals would be awarded to teams as well as to individuals. This meant that the less sporty in a class would also feel involved and have the chance to win an Olympic medal.

Planning the timetable raised the interesting effects of timelines, and date lines and involved the pupils in a variety of mathematical and geographical activities in a real life context. Language activities had more meaning as the pupils saw purpose and reason in them. They distributed information about themselves, their school and city, and through communication with the other schools were reading for information and becoming more aware of the need for clarity in their own writing. Interest was stimulated in foreign languages as they gathered a range of useful phrases from the other schools.

The pupils added their event logo, mascot and anthem to the Home Page and world wide publication gave a sense of pride and satisfaction.

The competition

By far the most exciting aspect of the project was the actual competition itself. The pupils carried out a great deal of research into health, diet and fitness training in preparation for the competition and this covered a wide range of Science and PE.

Once the competition was underway the pupils videoed their own events and short pieces of film were added to the Home Page, allowing the pupils around the world to share in each others' events. Tape recordings of commentary for events were also included.

Results

Each school was required to pass on their results as soon as their events were completed and there was a great deal of excitement as these came in. This interest and excitement made the mathematics of recording the information, interpreting and displaying it an enjoyable one and made the mathematics more meaningful. The organising school had the responsibility of producing the on-line news report of each event and display of the results. Each competing school also sent details of climatic conditions at the time of the event in their school, which was a fascinating up-to-the-minute source of information for a study of weather. All data collected was accessible through the Web Page.

The information from the competing pupils around the world allowed comparison of the heights, weights and speeds of pupils with those of the same age from different countries, and the pupils investigated whether there were any similarities between the food intake of pupils and their growth.

The opportunity of world wide publication was a great stimulus for language work and a great deal of discussion took place on the best way to display results and the layout of pages.

Closing ceremony

At the end of the competition the pupils found it interesting to compare the achievements of the Cyberspace Olympic countries with those of the actual Olympics. The project ended with photographs of medal winners being added to the Internet. On the page which displayed the individual and team winner of an event there was an opportunity to hear the National Anthem of the winner, and the Games Mascot was dressed in the national costume of the winner's country.

Question

The Olympics is a sporting event which could inspire inter-school competition and associated topic work. What other sporting events could be used to inspire your pupils? Events such as Wimbledon or the World Cup could not be organised in exactly the same way as the work inspired by the Olympics, but is there still scope for inter-school competition? What work *could* be inspired by such events?

Internet support for the topic

Language

Posters

Official Olympic Web Page:

http://www.olympic.org

Attracting other participants

Spanish Schools:
http://www.worldwide.edu/ci/spain/index.html

French Schools:
http://www.worldwide.edu/ci/france/index.html

Hong Kong Schools:
http://www.worldwide.edu/index.html

Newsgroups:
news:k12.chat.teacher

Web newspaper

Creating Web pages:
http://web66.coled.umn.edu/Cookbook/contents.html

Reference skills

Ancient World Wide Web:
http://atlantic.evsc.virginia.edu/Julia/AncientWorld.html

Other languages

Human languages page:
http://www.dcs.warwick.ac.uk/~bear/Language-Page.html

Mathematics

Currency

Exchange Rates:
http://www.dna.lth.se/cgi-bin/kurt/rates/

Records and comparisons

Current sporting records:
http://www.hkkk.fi/~niinien/athl.html

Physical Education

Fitness training

Advice on health & fitness:
http://segment.ucsf.edu/brent/fitness/fitness.htm

Science

Our bodies

http://sin.fi.edu/biosci/heart.html

Diet

http://www.hoptechno.com/rdindex.htm

Animal athletes

http://izzy.online.discovery.com/DCO/doc

Geography

Climate

http://www.meto.govt.uk

Information about countries

http://www.countries.com

Host cities:
http://www.venus.net/~nwashel2/host.cities.html

Travel

http://wings.buffalo.edu/world/vt2/

History

Ancient Greece

The Olympic Games in Ancient Greece:

http://www.venus.net/nwashel2/ancient.greece.html

http://www.auspart.gov.au/anc.html

The Olympic Games:
http://www.auspart.gov.au/olymenu.html

The Glory of Olympia:
http://www-adm.pdx.edu/user/sinq/greekciv/jeannie1.html

Politics of Olympic Games

Mexico Olympics – 1968:
http://www.welwyngymbook.com/mexico.htm

The Olympic Games in Modern Times:
http://www.venus.net/~nwashel2/modern.times.html

http://www.france.diplomatie.fr/

Art and Design

Flags

http://www.adfa.oz.au/CS/flg/index.html

National dress

http://www.taisbean.com/celticnet/kilthistory.html

Mascots

http://www.worldgames.com/olympics/

General information

Olympic Games Information:
http://www.venus.net/~nwashel2/olympic.games.html

Official 1996 Olympic web site:
http://www.olympic.org

Authentic Olympic Games Collection:
http://www.worldgames.com/olympics/

For further help in designing your project we have included two worksheets which can be found on pages 103 and 104.

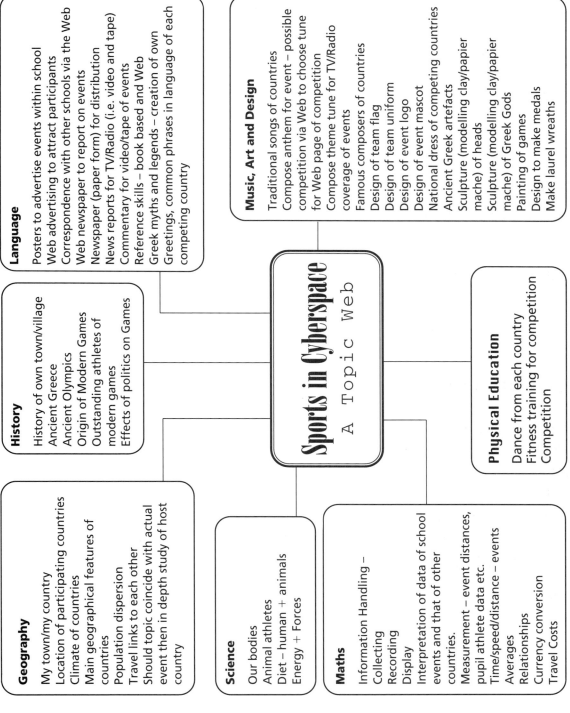

Language

Posters to advertise events within school
Web advertising to attract participants
Correspondence with other schools via the Web
Web newspaper to report on events
Newspaper (paper form) for distribution
News reports for TV/Radio (i.e. video and tape)
Commentary for video/tape of events
Reference skills – book based and Web
Greek myths and legends – creation of own
Greetings, common phrases in language of each competing country

Music, Art and Design

Traditional songs of countries
Compose anthem for event – possible competition via Web to choose tune for Web page of competition
Compose theme tune for TV/Radio coverage of events
Famous composers of countries
Design of team flag
Design of team uniform
Design of event logo
Design of event mascot
National dress of competing countries
Ancient Greek artefacts
Sculpture (modelling clay/papier mache) of heads
Sculpture (modelling clay/papier mache) of Greek Gods
Painting of games
Design to make medals
Make laurel wreaths

History

History of own town/village
Ancient Greece
Ancient Olympics
Origin of Modern Games
Outstanding athletes of modern games
Effects of politics on Games

Sports in Cyberspace
A Topic Web

Physical Education

Dance from each country
Fitness training for competition
Competition

Geography

My town/my country
Location of participating countries
Climate of countries
Main geographical features of countries
Population dispersion
Travel links to each other
Should topic coincide with actual event then in depth study of host country

Science

Our bodies
Animal athletes
Diet – human + animals
Energy + Forces

Maths

Information Handling –
Collecting
Recording
Display
Interpretation of data of school events and that of other countries.
Measurement – event distances, pupil athlete data etc.
Time/speed/distance – events
Averages
Relationships
Currency conversion
Travel Costs

This page is photocopiable

Chapter 6

Raiders and invaders: A study of the Vikings

Introduction

As people in past times travelled into and invaded other countries they left behind evidence of their own culture. Today in Britain our cultural, linguistic and literary inheritance reveals the influence of various other peoples. One group of people which made a lasting impact were the Vikings.

This chapter explains how the Internet can support a study of the Vikings, and allows pupils to reach sources and people that previously would not have been readily accessible.

Case Study: The Vikings

A class were preparing for a visit to York and their class teacher told them a little about the history of the city. The children were particularly interested in the fact

that the Vikings had been there. As a follow up to the lesson on the city, the teacher printed out 'Valhalla', a poem by Ælfric Halfdansson, which is on the Internet. This was used as a stimulus for discussion and investigation into the life of the Vikings as described in this example.

After reading and discussing the poem the pupils were set the task of finding out where the Vikings lived and whether they had visited countries other than our own. The teacher directed them to the Viking Network site which has a wealth of information presented at a suitable reading age for the pupils. From this site the children were instructed to find out which were the Vikings' home countries and to print out a map which showed the different areas of the world visited by the Vikings.

The Viking Network Site:
http://odin.nls.no/viking/e/ehome.htm

The poem 'Valhalla':
http://www.ftech.net/~regia/valhalla.htm

At home with the Vikings

Now that the children knew where the Vikings lived, the class then investigated their home life and were able to find information on Viking furniture, homes, food and clothing at the Viking Network site. The teacher also printed out information on these subjects from other sources on the Internet and these were used as resource sheets for the pupils.

The poem 'Valhalla' concentrates on the Vikings as raiders but also refers to them returning home to their loved ones. This led to a discussion as to what everyday life would be like for the Vikings. A study of the role of Viking women and children was undertaken. The teacher created worksheets which contained questions the children could answer by referring to the Viking Network site.

The Jorvik Internet site, created by the Jorvik Centre in York, was useful as it takes the pupils through a Viking village and highlights some of the trades that were practised there. From the Regia Anglorum site dealing with the history of early Britain, pages can be visited which explain in detail Viking Crafts including leather work, weaving, copper work, jewellery, woodwork and bone work, and indeed step-by-step instructions on how to make a Viking shoe can be found. The children tried to weave in the Viking way and made a Viking shoe from felt. With reference to a site on Viking jewellery the children designed and created their own pendants and brooches.

The teacher also printed out a plan of a Viking village which showed how the houses were constructed and this was used to support the children in the creation of a model Viking village.

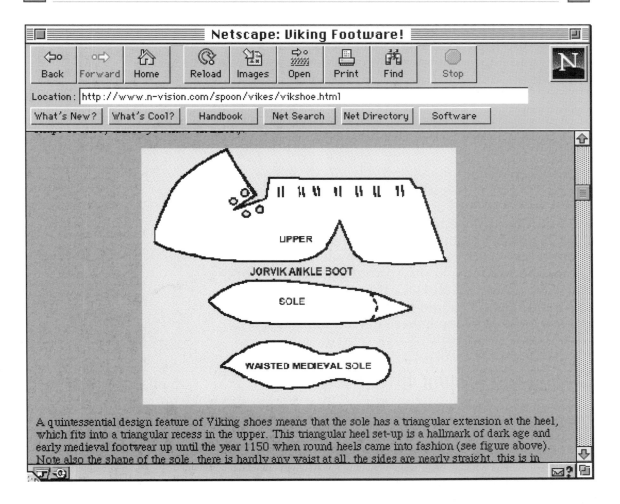

A quintessential design feature of Viking shoes means that the sole has a triangular extension at the heel, which fits into a triangular recess in the upper. This triangular heel set-up is a hallmark of dark age and early medieval footwear up until the year 1150 when round heels came into fashion (see figure above). Note also the shape of the sole, there is hardly any waist at all, the sides are nearly straight, this is in

The Jorvik Centre:
http://www.demon.co.uk/tourism/jvc/never.html

Graphics of jewellery:
http://www.eskimo.com/~revoke/index.html

Lucets (cord making):
http://www.ftech.net/~regia/lucets.htm

Basic Guide to Footwear in the Viking Age:
http://www.n-vision.com/spoon/vikes/vikshoe.html

Internet sites contain details about foods of the Vikings and the plants and animals in Britain at that time. An interesting nature/wildlife table was created where the children displayed a selection of branches, plants, flowers and photographs of animals the Vikings would have known and which are still to be found today.

Fun and games with the Vikings

A discussion about how Viking warriors would be selected led to an investigation into the sports and games of the Vikings and the children tried out some of the safer sports – the teacher thought it unwise to have them compete in drowning each other to find the stronger of a pair! The pupils also made some of the games and tried them out. Again the Viking Network site was the most suitable for the majority of pupils in terms of reading age and presentation of the material, but the more able pupils were guided to other sites.

Raiding and trading with the Vikings

The poem 'Valhalla' tells of the Viking dragon ships and the children found interesting information on what their ships looked like and followed the routes they would have taken on the map that had been printed earlier. Graphics of ships were printed out and used as a guide for art work and model making. Researching how the Vikings travelled led to some fascinating discoveries about the navigational aids used by the Vikings – apparently fleas were taken from a Viking's hair or clothes and placed on the tiller to point the way as fleas always hop towards the North! Although there are many Internet sites relating to Viking voyages the Viking Network site was sufficient for most pupils. However, the teacher also printed out information from other sites and these were available for pupils who wanted more detail.

From the Viking Network site the children visited each of the countries to which the Vikings had travelled. At

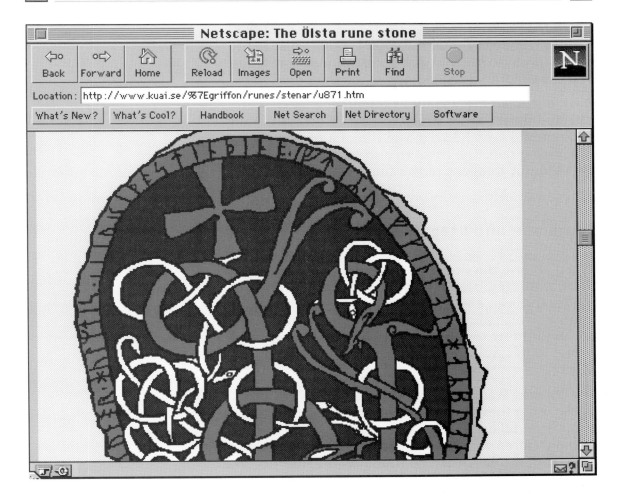

the North American site they found an interesting selection of Viking raps which inspired the children to try out their own composing talents! At the Icelandic site the children were able to listen to an Icelandic child speaking in the language of the Vikings.

As the children visited each country that the Vikings had visited they discovered that they had not only been raiders but also traders, and investigated what benefits there would be for the Vikings and those countries. The children were intrigued by the fact that many of the Vikings settled in the countries they visited. This led the children to look at place names in the countries to which they had gone to search for evidence that the Vikings had been there. A study of trading also led to the children finding out about currency at that time and the children designed and made their own coins.

Having studied the Vikings as traders the teacher directed them to sites which contained details of raids, and one site even had a movie clip of a reconstruction of a Viking raid. The children also found a wealth of detail about weapons of this time.

Language and literature

When visiting the site of Miklagard (now Istanbul), there was reference to graffiti left by the Vikings and the teacher was able to take a rune font from the Internet which allowed the children to use their word processor to write in runes. They enjoyed writing their names in this way and sending coded messages to each other.

The children wanted to know if the Vikings wrote books using these runes and the teacher explained about storytellers. Viking stories were printed and read to the children who then wrote their own. The story of 'The Forging', which can be found on the Internet, was read to the children and used as a stimulus for a discussion on not judging people by appearances. They then carried out an exercise where each pupil's name was written on a separate piece of paper and these were then circulated. Everyone had to write a good point or strength about the person named. Each child kept his or her list of good points.

Worshipping with the Vikings

The poem 'Valhalla', which the teacher had read to the children, talks of the Viking gods and the idea of Valhalla. The teacher printed out details of the worlds of the gods and the children created paintings of how they thought these would be. A study of the gods also informed the children of the link of our days of the week to the Vikings.

Viking quizzes

To complete the topic the children completed both the beginners and the expert quizzes to be found at the Viking Network site. This is an excellent way of allowing the pupils to develop their browsing skills. All of the answers are within the Viking Network site and the pupils find their way to the answers by clicking on hypertext links. The children will by now have a good idea of what the majority of the pages contain and will therefore be less likely to go down the wrong route just to find out what is there! This is a temptation for everyone who uses the Internet at first and can become quite a costly exercise.

Further development

There are opportunities, via links, to use electronic mail to gather information from people in other areas and countries, about the Viking influences or artefacts to be found there. The example described above was carried out by a class in an area which did not have any close Viking links. If your school is located in an area where there is evidence of Viking influence then you might like to take advantage of the Viking Network E-mail projects. These allow the children to gather and present information about their local area's history which the Viking Network Team will present on the Web. This gives the added dimension of global publishing. Full details of how to go about this are included at the Viking Network site.

Question

How much would this topic inspire and motivate your pupils? Which elements would be most likely to capture their imagination? What are the main outcomes which you would expect to see being developed in your classroom? What would *your* aims and *your* objectives be if you decided to run this topic as described? Are you convinced that the costs, both in terms of your time and the school's money, can be justified on educational grounds?

Internet support for the topic

As explained in the case study the Viking Network site is very valuable for pupil use. It is possible to direct the pupils there and then allow them to navigate their way to the necessary pages within the site. If your children are fairly inexperienced or access time and cost are a consideration, then you can give your pupils the Uniform Resource Locator for specific pages. The quiz at the end of the project would then allow the pupils the freedom to browse. For this reason the Uniform Resource Locator for the Viking Network site is included and also those for the individual pages within this site. The World of the Vikings, The Vikings (NFPS) and Viking Heritage have lots of interesting information, but some of this would have to be used by the teacher to create resources rather than be used on-line by the pupils because of the reading age. These sites have links to other pages and the Uniform Resource Locators will be given in the following section for the main pages of these sites and also for specific pages under subject headings.

Sites with links to a variety of information

Viking Network Site

Starting off point for children:
http://odin.nls.no/viking/e/ehome.htm

Viking Network Site

Information on joining and e-mail projects:
http://odin.nls.no/viking/vnet/e/evnet.htm

The Vikings (NFPS):
http://www.biochem.ucl.ac.uk/~davis/vikings.html

Viking Heritage:
http://bull.got.kth.se/~viking/index.html

World of the Vikings:
http://pastforward.co.uk/vikings/index.

Regia Anglorum:
http://www.ftech.net/~regia/

Being Creative – Everyday Life in a Viking Village:
http://www.to.utwente.nl/ism/online96/project/kiosk/team5/bc05.htm

The Vikings:
http://www.n-vision.com/spoon/vikes/index.html

Art

History of ornamentation in Viking Art:
http://www.n-vision.com/spoon/vikes/vikorn.html

Page of jewellery links with good clear graphics:
http://www.eskimo.com/~revoke/index.html

Graphics

Viking Image Gallery:
http://www.biochem.ucl.ac.uk/~davis/images/gallery.html

Links to interesting photos:
http://www.control.chalmers.se/vikings/LVS/lvs.html

Graphics of jewellery:
http://www.eskimo.com/~revoke/index.html

This is a quiz site but contains excellent graphics:
http://bull.got.kth.se/~viking/Quizshow.html

A Viking raid (A short movie clip can be viewed here):
http://odin.nls.no/viking/images/naerkamp.mpg

Picture of a house:
http://www.biochem.ucl.ac.uk/~davis/images/weststow.jpg

Language

English/Swedish/Viking Dictionary of words:
http://www.control.chalmers.se/vikings/LVS/dictionary.html

Do you speak Viking? Listen to an Icelandic child speak:
http://odin.nls.no/viking/e/heritage/evoices.htm

Placenames. Links from this page to information on placenames in a variety
of countries:
http://odin.nls.no/viking/e/heritage/eplacenames/placenames.htm

Language:
http://www.ftech.net/~regia/languag.htm

Towns, villages, homes, furniture, household items

The Jorvik Centre:
http://www.demon.co.uk/tourism/jvc/never.html

Houses, villages and towns:
http://www.biochem.ucl.ac.uk/~davis/housing.html

Houses and furniture:
http://www.ftech.net/~regia/houses.htm

The Longhouse:
http://odin.nls.no/viking/e/life/elonghouses.htm

Household items:
http://www.biochem.ucl.ac.uk/~davis/items.html

Social structure, law and order

Role of women and children:
http://odin.nls.no/viking/e/life/ewomen.htm

Viking social organisation:
http://www.ftech.net/~regia/viking2.htm

Viking status:
http://www.n-vision.com/spoon/vikes/vikstat.html

The Vikings and the law:
http://odin.nls.no/viking/e/life/elaws.htm

Clothing

Clothes:
http://odin.nls.no/viking/e/life/eclothes.htm

A Basic Guide to Footwear in the Viking Age:
http://www.n-vision.com/spoon/vikes/vikshoe.html

Clothing:
http://www.biochem.ucl.ac.uk/~davis/clothing.html

Food and drink

The Viking diet:
http://odin.nls.no/viking/e/life/efood.htm

Feasting and fasting:
http://www.ftech.net/~regia/feasting.htm

Food and drink:
http://www.ftech.net/~regia/food.htm

Food:
http://www.biochem.ucl.ac.uk/~davis/food.html

Crafts

Bone and antler working:
http://www.ftech.net/~regia/bonework.htm

Bronze working:
http://www.ftech.net/~regia/bronzwrk.htm

Woodworking:
http://www.ftech.net/~regia/woodwork.htm

Glass and amber:
http://www.ftech.net/~regia/glass.htm

Metal working:
http://www.ftech.net/~regia/othmetwk.htm

Leather work:
http://www.ftech.net/~regia/leatwork.htm

Embroidery techniques:
http://www.ftech.net/~regia/embroid.htm

Sprang (intricate plaiting):
http://www.ftech.net/~regia/sprang.htm

Lucets (cord making):
http://www.ftech.net/~regia/lucets.htm

Nalebinding:
http://www.ftech.net/~regia/naalbind.htm

Wool and stuff:
http://www.ftech.net/~regia/textile1.htm

Textile:
http://www.ftech.net/~regia/textiles.htm

Currency

The Vikings and money in England:
http://odin.nls.no/viking/e/heritage/emoney.htm

Vikings in Norway make their own coins:
http://odin.nls.no/viking/e/heritage/en-money.htm

For what it's worth:
http://www.ftech.net/~regia/costs.htm

Fauna and flora

Fauna:
http://www.ftech.net/~regia/fauna.htm

Vegetation and flora:
http://www.ftech.net/~regia/flora.htm

Trade, ships and travel

Viking trade:
http://odin.nls.no/viking/e/travels/etrade.htm

Trading, exports and imports:
http://www.biochem.ucl.ac.uk/~davis/trading.html

Vikings:
http://www.ftech.net/~regia/vikings.htm

The Vikings ships, contains links to information about longships and Viking merchant ships:

http://odin.nls.no/viking/e/travels/evikingships.htm

On the high seas, contains links to navigational aids, preparations taken before setting sail and a map showing how the Vikings sailed from Norway to Greenland:

http://odin.nls.no/viking/e/travels/navigation/e-highsea.htm

Up and down the coast:

http://odin.nls.no/viking/e/travels/navigation/e-updown.htm

Problems encountered:

http://odin.nls.no/viking/e/travels/navigation/e-proble.htm

Navigation instruments:

http://odin.nls.no/viking/e/travels/navigation/e-instru.htm

The Viking world. Links on this page take you to fact sheets on the countries:

http://odin.nls.no/viking/e/maps/emaps.htm

Weapons and warfare

Dark age combat – contains details of weapons, combat style and tactics:

http://www.biochem.ucl.ac.uk/~davis/combat.html

Viking military organisation:

http://www.ftech.net/~regia/viking3.htm

Guthorm's invasion of Wessex. By clicking on links the children can follow the story from 877 to 879:

http://odin.nls.no/viking/e/england/guttorm/e-introduction.htm

Sports and games

The Vikings and sport. This page within the Viking Network site has links to a variety of Viking sports. Reading age and presentation suitable for pupils and easy to navigate:

http://odin.nls.no/viking/e/life/sports/esports.htm

Games of the Viking and Anglo Saxon Age:
http://www.ftech.net/~regia/games.htm

Pastimes of The Viking and Anglo Saxon Age:
http://www.ftech.net/~regia/pastimes.htm

The spear game:
http://cougarnet.byu.edu/acd1/ed/InSci/286/search/SearchSpear.html # game

Music, verse and stories

Fun raps and songs:
http://odin.nls.no/viking/info-sheets/usa/rap.htm

Valhalla – poem:
http://www.ftech.net/~regia/valhalla.htm

The Forging:
http://www.ftech.net/~regia/forging.htm

Othere's Voyage to the White Sea:
http://odin.nls.no/viking/e/travels/navigation/e-ottar.htm

Nordic Mythology:
http://www.luth.se/luth.se/luth/present/sweden/history/gods/Old_ norse_myth.html

Music and verse:
http://www.ftech.net/~regia/music.htm

Religious Education

List of Norse Beings:
http://www.ugcs.caltech.edu/~cherryne/list.html

The Nine Worlds. From here it is possible to visit pages on each of the nine worlds:
http://www.ugcs.caltech.edu/~cherryne/worlds.html

The Viking Gods:
http://odin.nls.no/viking/e/life/egods.htm

The Vikings meet Christianity:
http://odin.nls.no/viking/e/life/echristianity.htm

Blot (A sacrifice):
http://odin.nls.no/viking/e/life/eblot.htm

Quizzes

The Viking Heritage Quiz. If the children give the correct answer to the questions they can then click on the word 'picture' and an interesting photograph or drawing of the answer will be displayed, for instance a photograph of a Viking helmet. These graphics can be saved and used in their written reports:
http://bull.got.kth.se/~viking/Quizshow.html

Viking Network Beginners Quiz:
http://odin.nls.no/viking/problems/equiz-beginners.htm

Viking Network Expert Quiz:
http://odin.nls.no/viking/problems/equiz-experts.htm

Viking Network Viking Maths Beginners Quiz:
http://odin.nls.no/viking/problems/ematteb.htm

Viking Network Viking Maths Expert Quiz:
http://odin.nls.no/viking/problems/emattee.htm

Runes

Background to runes:
http://www.kuai.se/%7Egriffon/runes/

Runes:
http://odin.nls.no/viking/e/heritage/eruner.htm

Runic Font for Apple Macintosh Computers:
http://babel.uoregon.edu/Yamada/fonts/runes.html

Runic Fonts:
http://www.pastforward.co.uk/vikings/runes.html

General background information

Viking Timeline:
http://odin.nls.no/viking/e/etimeline.htm

Viking Age Timeline:
http://www.control.chalmers.se/vikings/LVS/historia.html

For further help in designing your project we have included two worksheets which can be found on pages 105 and 107.

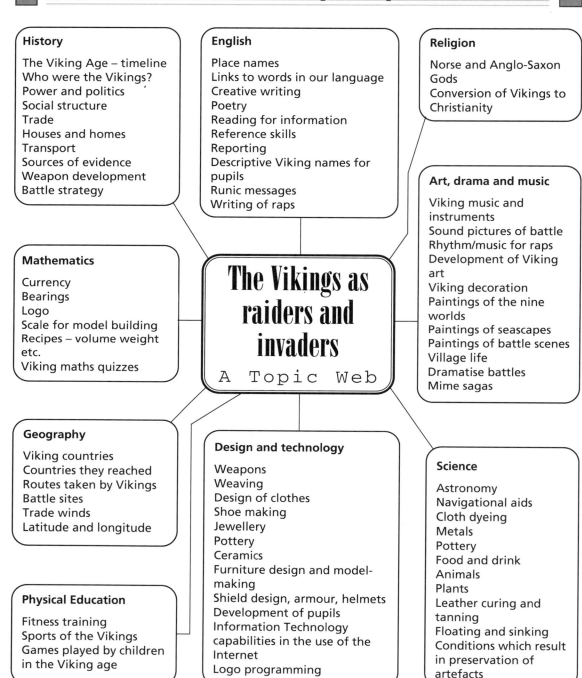

History

The Viking Age – timeline
Who were the Vikings?
Power and politics
Social structure
Trade
Houses and homes
Transport
Sources of evidence
Weapon development
Battle strategy

English

Place names
Links to words in our language
Creative writing
Poetry
Reading for information
Reference skills
Reporting
Descriptive Viking names for pupils
Runic messages
Writing of raps

Religion

Norse and Anglo-Saxon Gods
Conversion of Vikings to Christianity

Art, drama and music

Viking music and instruments
Sound pictures of battle
Rhythm/music for raps
Development of Viking art
Viking decoration
Paintings of the nine worlds
Paintings of seascapes
Paintings of battle scenes
Village life
Dramatise battles
Mime sagas

Mathematics

Currency
Bearings
Logo
Scale for model building
Recipes – volume weight etc.
Viking maths quizzes

The Vikings as raiders and invaders

A Topic Web

Geography

Viking countries
Countries they reached
Routes taken by Vikings
Battle sites
Trade winds
Latitude and longitude

Design and technology

Weapons
Weaving
Design of clothes
Shoe making
Jewellery
Pottery
Ceramics
Furniture design and model-making
Shield design, armour, helmets
Development of pupils Information Technology capabilities in the use of the Internet
Logo programming

Science

Astronomy
Navigational aids
Cloth dyeing
Metals
Pottery
Food and drink
Animals
Plants
Leather curing and tanning
Floating and sinking
Conditions which result in preservation of artefacts

Physical Education

Fitness training
Sports of the Vikings
Games played by children in the Viking age

This page is photocopiable

Chapter 7
An ancient civilisation: The Aztecs

Introduction

Studying ancient civilisations develops a respect for other cultures, an awareness of place and time and an understanding of the effects of the past on the present. The influence of one culture on another and its impact are important lessons for everyone.

The Ancient civilisations of South America are a fascinating area of study. The colour and spectacle of their ceremonies and the imposing structures of their cities capture the imagination of young and old alike. This chapter will illustrate how this interest can be harnessed and used as a stimulus for a cross-curricular study of the Aztecs. A topic web is included on page 74.

Carrying out an Aztec project

Allowing pupils to browse the Internet in the hope of
locating suitable sites could be expensive and time
consuming. Teachers should therefore pre-select a
number of sites which can be linked to the specific topic
studied. Care should be taken to ensure that these are
suited to the needs of the pupils in terms of reading
age, suitability of content and theme. The sites could
also be grouped according to the curricular headings
given on the topic web.

an ancient civilisation: the aztecs

Set the pupils the task of discovering who the Aztecs were and why they settled where they did. A page on the pre-colonial history of Mexico gives a wealth of information on this.

Mexico: Pre-Colonial history:
http://www.lonelyplanet.com.au/dest/cam/mexhis.htm

Where did they live?

Direct pupils to the page entitled the Aztec Environment where they can find out where the Aztecs lived. They can then look at maps of the world, both on and off-line, and find South America and Mexico. This could lead to a study of the climate of the area today and a comparison with the climate during the time of the Aztecs. From this same page they will learn about the fertility of the soil and the irrigation systems used by the Aztecs.

There are many places on the Internet for the children to find out about where the Aztecs settled. One of the real advantages of accessing information from the Internet, as opposed to finding out from books, is that the information is up to date and any recent discoveries can be instantly discussed. An interesting site to visit is GB Online's Mesoamerica. Here it is possible to view archaeological sites and, through recent discoveries, experience everyday Aztec life, their settlements, buildings, food and clothes.

Time waits for no man

When accessing information about the lives of the Aztecs, the pupils will discover some very interesting sites about the calendars they used. These sites not only display the beautiful Calendar Stones, but they also tell them how to interpret the calendars. Indeed on one site it is possible to download an Aztec Calendar program which can then be used to translate birthdays into Aztec dates, complete with authentic Aztec glyphs!

The Aztec Calendar for MacOS:

http://www.xs4all.nl/~voorburg/aztec.html

On one of these sites it is possible not only to see a very colourful example of an Aztec Calendar, but also to listen to the names of the months in the Aztec language of Nahuatl. This same page also contains a list of the names of the months, so the pronunciation of the months can be linked with their written form.

This can act as a stimulus for a great deal of art work. Calendar Stones can be designed using the glyphs found on the Aztec Calendar program. Many of the sites have pictorial evidence of the Aztec way of life. Some are photographs of buildings that have survived and others are Aztec drawings. These can either be used as a stimulus or downloaded and incorporated into resources.

What did they believe?

The Aztecs worshipped many gods. There are some interesting sites on the Internet relating to Aztec religion and astronomy, but some of these can lead to very grim discoveries about the human sacrifices and the lives of the priests. These should therefore be handled with sensitivity.

Other religions in the world at the time of the Aztecs also feature on the Internet. Some of the sites visited will lead to discussions about the ancient civilisations of the world and whether they were known to each other.

Why did they disappear?

The Aztecs were a very powerful civilisation so why did they not survive? This question can be answered by accessing sites with information about the Spanish Conquest, the arrival of Cortes, Montezuma and the fall of the Aztec civilisation.

The Internet advantage

An advantage in using the Internet for this topic is that the children do not need to leave their classroom! Much of the data that the pupils discover comes from America and from many sources that the children would otherwise find difficult to reach. A rich variety of nformation can be accessed (not only text, but graphics and sounds) and be collected for use in their own displays and reports. On-line quizzes can add to the fun.

Question

What new work could be developed as a result of the work on this topic? What other curricular areas such as English or Music could be the centre of an Internet topic? From your experience of using the Internet what could it add to such a curricular area?

Internet support for the topic

Expressive Arts

Buildings

University of Guadalajara page on Mexico:
http://mexico.udg.mx/ingles.html

The Aztecs/Mexicas:
http://www.indians.org/welker/aztec.htm

Ancient City of Teotihuacan:
http://www.lonelyplanet.com/au/dest/cam/graphics/mex21.htm

Calendars

The Famous Aztec Calendar Stone:
http://copan.bioz.unibas.ch/meso/sunstone.jpg

How are the prehispanic calendars interpreted?:
http://www.public.iastate.edu/~rjsalvad/scmfaq/calendar.html

The Mexican Heritage Almanac:
http://www.ironhorse.com/~nagual/alma.html

Culture and society of Mexico:
http://www.public.iastate.edu/~rjsalvad/scmfaq/scmfaq.html

Mesoamerican calendars:
http://www.mexico-virtual.com/~nagual/calendar/

Ancient writings

Ancient Mesoamerican Writing:
http://pages.prodigy.com/GBonline/ancwrite-old.html awaztec

The Aztec Calendar for MacOS:
http://www.xs4all.nl/~voorburg/aztec.html

Aztec Books, documents and writing:
http://www.azteca.net/aztec/nahuatl/writing.html

Costumes

Mesoamerica:
http://www.burbank.k12.ca.us/~luther/aztecs/azsiclot.html

Graphics

Aztec coloring book:
http://www.burbank.k12.ca.us/~luther/aztecs/azcolorbk/azcolorbk.html

Physical Education

Patolli – Aztec Game:
http://www.azteca.net/aztec/nahuatl/game.shtml

Science

Astronomy

Lords of the Earth: Maya/Aztec/Inca Center:
http://www.realtime.net/maya/

Mesoamerica:
http://www.indians.org/welker/aztecs.htm

Climate

Mesoamerica:
http://www.public.iastate.edu/~rjsalvad/scmfaq/weather.html

Food

Mesoamerica:
http://www.burbank.k12.ca.us/~luther/aztecs/azsifood.html

FAQ on Mexican culture:
http://www.public.iastate.edu/~rjsalvad/scmfaq/faqindex.html

Aztec food and drink:
http://k12.colostate.edu/~gmoreno/AZTEC_FOOD_DRINK.html

History

Origins

Mexico: Pre-Colonial History:
http://www.lonelyplanet.com.au/dest/cam/mexhis.htm

Origins of Mexico:
http://www.azteca.net/aztec/mexica.html

Mexicana: The Aztecs:
http://www.mexicana.com/english/community/29nf-aztec.shtml

The Aztecs (1300–1519):
http://riceinfo.rice.edu/armadillo/Schools/HSHP/aztec.html

The Aztecs:
http://www.rmplc.co.uk/eduweb/sites/wickham/topics/aztecs/aztecs.html

Learn about the Aztecs:
ttp://www.burbank.k12.ca.us/~luther/aztecs/azlearn.html

Politics

The Aztecs/Mexicas:
http://www.indians.org/welker/aztec.htm

University of Guadalajara page on Mexico:
http://mexico.udg.mx/ingles.html

The Aztecs/Mexicas:
http://www.indians.org/welker/aztec.htm

Mesoamerica:
http://kira.pomona.claremont.edu/mesoamerica.html

Pre-conquest civilisations:
http://www.itsnet.com/home/asumnall/latam/notes/la1.html

Social classes

Pre-conquest civilisations:
ttp://www.itsnet.com/home/asumnall/latam/notes/la1.html

Mesoamerica:
http://kira.pomona.claremont.edu/mesoamerica.html

FAQ on Mexican culture:
http://www.public.iastate.edu/~rjsalvad/scmfaq/faqindex.html

Social organisation of the Aztecs:
http://www.azteca.net/aztec/nahuatl/organiza.html

Social organisation:
**http://udgftp.cencar.udg.mx/ingles/Precolumbina/Azteca/
organizacionsoc.html**

Economy

Mesoamerica: **http://kira.pomona.claremont.edu/mesoamerica.html**

Pre-conquest civilisations:
http://www.itsnet.com/home/asumnall/latam/notes/la1.html

Invasion of Cortes

Mexico: Pre-Colonial history:
http://www.lonelyplanet.com.au/dest/cam/mexhis.htm

The Aztecs:
http://www.eecs.uic.edu/~jgarcia/Aztecs.html

Pre-conquest civilisations:
http://www.itsnet.com/home/asumnall/latam/notes/la1.html

The Spanish invade:
http://knet.kingsnet.com/users/recardo/pictures/Spanish.html

Montezuma's Buried Royal Cache:
http://floyd.xpressweb.com/kanab/montezuma.html

Language

Nahuatl

The Aztecs/Mexicas:
http://www.indians.org/welker/aztec.htm

Mesoamerica:
http://kira.pomona.claremont.edu/mesoamerica.html

How are the pre-hispanic calendars interpreted?:
http://www.public.iastate.edu/~rjsalvad/scmfaq/calendar.html

FAQ on Mexican culture:
http://www.public.iastate.edu/~rjsalvad/scmfaq/faqindex.html

The Nahuatl language of the Aztecs:
http://www.indians.org/welker/nahuatl.htm

Nahuatl placenames

Some Nahuatl placenames:
http://www.azteca.net/aztec/nahuatl/placenam.html

Poetry

Aztec poems:
http://www.indians.org/welker/aztpoem.htm

A Pre-Columbian Mexico poem:
http://www.indians.org/welker/mexpoet.htm

Quizzes

The Aztecs (1300–1519):
http://riceinfo.rice.edu/armadillo/Schools/HSHP/aztec.html

Aztecs – QUIZ:
http://www.burbank.k12.ca.us/~luther/aztecs/azqui1.html

Creative writing

Aztec historical fiction:
http://www.burbank.k12.ca.us/~luther/aztecs/azhfak.html

Religious Education

The Aztecs/Mexicas:
http://www.indians.org/welker/aztec.htm

Pre-conquest civilisations:
http://www.itsnet.com/home/asumnall/latam/notes/la1.html

The Aztecs/Mexicas:
http://www.indians.org/welker/aztec.htm

Lords of the Earth:
http://www.realtime.net/maya/

The Sun Stone:
http://www.lalc.k12.ca.us/laep/smart/Sunrise/sunstone.html

Aztecs and their beliefs:
**http://pen1.pen.k12.va.us/Anthology/Div/Albemarle/Schools/
MurrayElem/ClassPages/Prudhomme/Explorers/aztec.html**

Aztec Creation Story:
http://www.indians.org/welker/aztecs.htm

Mathematics

How are the pre-hispanic calendars interpreted?:
http://www.public.iastate.edu/~rjsalvad/scmfaq/faqindex.html

Geography

Mesoamerica:
http://kira.pomona.claremont.edu/mesoamerica.html

Map of Mexico:
http://www.public.iastate.edu/~rjsalvad/scmfaq/images/map.gif

General Aztec Information Sites

Maya related WWW links:
http://www.astro.uva.nl/michielb/maya/links.html

The AZTECS Home Page:
http://www.burbank.k12.ca.us/~luther/aztecs/aztec.html

Arts, culture and history: Ancient Mexico: Aztec World:
http://www.trace-sc.com/aztec.htm

Nahuatl culture:
http://www.azteca.net/aztec/nahuatl/index.shtml

GB Online's Mesoamerica:
http://pages.prodigy.com/GBonline/mesowelc.html

**For further help with your project we have
included two worksheets which can be found on
pages 108 and 109.**

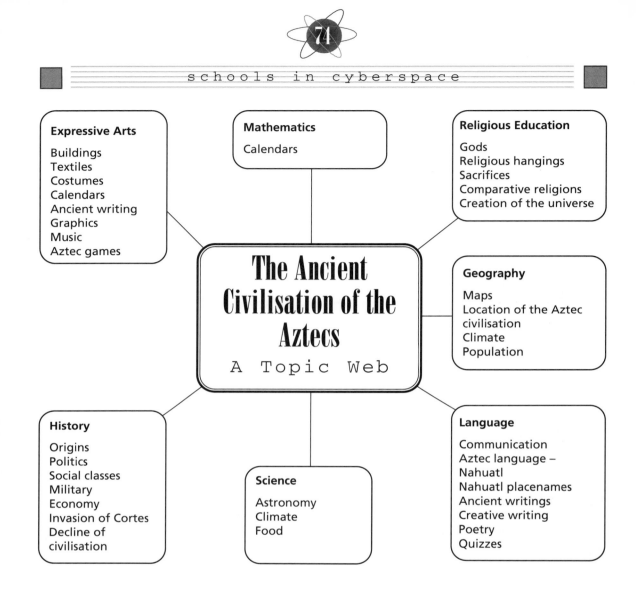

Expressive Arts

Buildings
Textiles
Costumes
Calendars
Ancient writing
Graphics
Music
Aztec games

Mathematics

Calendars

Religious Education

Gods
Religious hangings
Sacrifices
Comparative religions
Creation of the universe

The Ancient Civilisation of the Aztecs
A Topic Web

Geography

Maps
Location of the Aztec
civilisation
Climate
Population

History

Origins
Politics
Social classes
Military
Economy
Invasion of Cortes
Decline of
civilisation

Science

Astronomy
Climate
Food

Language

Communication
Aztec language –
Nahuatl
Nahuatl placenames
Ancient writings
Creative writing
Poetry
Quizzes

Chapter 8
Newspaper project

Introduction

A newspaper project is an ideal vehicle for language work and for developing Information Technology skills such as the use of word processors and desktop publishing. Such a project makes the idea of audience awareness more meaningful and allows exploration of genre within a real-life context.

The Internet allows pupils to increase their Information Technology skills, raise awareness of the differences between international and national news and develop a more critical approach to news coverage. The study of newspapers makes children more aware of current affairs, people and society, the influence of politics on the media and the media's power to influence opinion and control knowledge and information.

The following Case Study illustrates how a newspaper project was run in collaboration with schools in other countries, using the Internet for global communication, global collaboration, global publishing and as a global resource centre.

Case Study - World news

A teacher realised that a study of newspapers was an area of the curriculum where contact with schools around the world would enable the pupils to study current affairs, as well as gain an insight into what determines the importance of a news story.

The first stage was to establish contact with other interested schools and this was done by posting a message describing the project to a variety of newsgroups and mailing lists. There was no need to set a limit to the number of schools who could take part.

Each class involved in the project would undertake to study the news for one month. This study was limited to the newspapers and television coverage within their own country. The pupils took note of the most important and interesting items during that time. At the end of the month each participating class produced their own newspaper, which required minimal skill, and displayed it on the Internet. This newspaper was a summary of the news and features which they had gathered together during the previous month's study of the media.

These newspapers were printed and the pupils were able to study them for similarities and differences. Pupils were asked to consider why different countries emphasised different stories. This led to a discussion on political and cultural differences. On other occasions this could include a study of economic, political and geographical influences on the participating countries. Obviously the areas for discussion will vary each time this project is run depending on what is 'News' at the time.

This project offered a real-life context for language development. It provided opportunities for the study of current affairs and people and society. It also allowed the development of pupils' Information Technology capabilities.

Suggested stimulus

A study of people in the past can often stimulate an interest in the media. Children studying recent history, such as a topic on the Second World War, are often encouraged to interview members of their families about their memories of the war and the changes in their lives in the post-war era. This can prompt discussion about what is significant enough to be remembered in fifty years' time. Teachers can capitalise on the interest the children show in other people's memories of the past and suggest that the children should produce a record of this time in their lives to give future generations an insight.

Such a project would cover many aspects of the curriculum – local area study, collecting photographs, keeping diaries of their everyday lives – but the part of the project which will be looked at in more depth here is the study of news.

A study of the Second World War could make children more aware that the news printed in British newspapers at that time was not the same as that

printed in newspapers in Germany and could raise the question of differences today. (Many studies of the past could act as a similar stimulus.)

Two different methods of enabling your pupils to study the media from an international perspective are described here. The first method involves contacting other schools and results in your pupils publishing their own work globally. The second method does not require contact to be made with other pupils and results in your pupils publishing, using desktop publishing techniques, for a much smaller audience.

Carrying out the project: Method 1

Finding partners

To carry out a project similar to that described in the previous Case Study, you must first contact interested partners. To do so, prepare a short description of the project and display this on appropriate newsgroups and mailing lists. Allow time for contact to be made.

Studying the news

At the start of the project it is worth studying a range of newspapers. A recording sheet similar to the one on page 110 will help introduce your pupils to some of the vocabulary of newspapers, ways of establishing the importance of stories and indeed the different styles adopted by various newspapers.

Once your pupils start their study of the media, it will be necessary to have available a selection of each day's newspapers. (Speak nicely to your head teacher because this will cost a lot of money!) The pupils should be encouraged to continue their work at home by reading the newspapers read by their families and viewing early evening news programmes. They should then compare the headline stories of the morning newspapers with those given main coverage on evening television.

Summarising and publishing

At the end of each week there should be a class discussion of the stories gathered by the pupils and decisions made about which will be retained as possible items for the Internet newspaper they will produce.

At the end of one month you should display your newspaper on the Internet. Chapter 3 explains how you could achieve this. The creation of this newspaper will involve the pupils in design and layout as well as language development. To help your pupils in planning this presentation it would be worthwhile viewing a commercially produced newspaper on the Internet. A list of these is included in the Internet support section of this chapter.

Compare and contrast

Once the pupil Internet newspapers are created, each participating school will let the others know the

Uniform Resource Locator of their contribution and the comparison stage of the project can start. The Case Study described earlier, gives suggestions as to the possible discussion points. It is important for pupils to develop a critical approach to information and the media. Learning to detect bias and the ability to evaluate the trustworthiness of electronic sources of information are important skills which need to be developed.

Advantages and disadvantages

It can be difficult for pupils to cope with the reading level required for some newspapers, however one of the advantages of carrying out this study of international media is that rather than studying newspapers from other countries with unfamiliar cultures and vocabulary as well as an adult reading age, each participating country is studying their media and transforming it for other children to read and compare.

Carrying out the project: Method 2

This second method of carrying out the project involves the pupils in studying the media of a variety of countries at their original reading level. It does however allow the study of the media of non-English speaking countries, as many international newspapers publish English versions of their newspapers on the Internet. Viewing international newspapers on the Internet would be a valuable opportunity to raise the profile of other cultures and languages. It also allows a comparison of how long various stories remain newsworthy in countries. Method 1 may show that the same stories are covered, but does not show how quickly these were picked up by different countries – which can be one way of measuring the importance of stories involving other countries.

The Information Technology skills of you and your pupils will not need to include creating pages for the Internet; instead the Internet will be used as a library resource. Your pupils will develop their desktop publishing skills by working in groups to produce a newspaper for themselves and their peers.

Studying the news

The project should start with the study of newspapers using a sheet similar to that on page 110. As well as looking at ways of establishing the importance given to stories and the style of different papers, this initial session will develop knowledge of layout and

vocabulary of newspapers which will be valuable when the pupils come to prepare their own.

The children can study the newspapers read in their own homes and the news presented on television. The information they glean from these will be discussed in class. This starting point will raise the pupils' awareness of what stories are truly important, and those which merely have a sensationalist slant. The different stories gathered by the children can also help establish which newspapers are more likely to carry sensationalist stories and which ones the more serious news, and the different ways in which the same news story is presented.

Global links

To widen the study of the media to a global one, the children will access newspapers which are published on the Internet. How this is organised will very much depend on the amount of access time you have to the Internet and the budget constraints within which you must work.

Working in the established groups the children can access the Internet. If cost and access time are not restraints, then each group of children will access the newspapers on the Internet on a daily basis, making notes of the important stories and downloading any graphics which will be of use when producing their own papers.

You might prefer to have rotational responsibility for accessing the Internet. Groups will have responsibility for printing extracts from the newspapers found. The discussion will focus on the same points as the Case Study at the beginning of this chapter.

Hold the front page!

At the end of a month's study of the media, each group will produce a newspaper of the world news and the work can be compared. A list of the skills, knowledge and attitudes that working on such an exercise will help develop is included on page 112. You will probably be able to enlarge on this list.

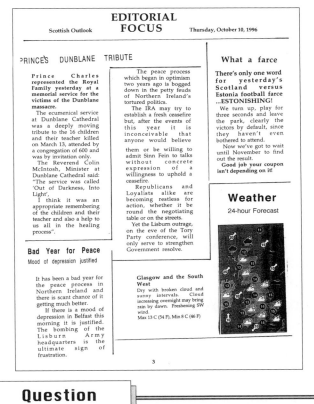

EDITORIAL FOCUS

Scottish Outlook   Thursday, October 10, 1996

PRINCE'S DUNBLANE TRIBUTE

Prince Charles represented the Royal Family yesterday at a memorial service for the victims of the Dunblane massacre.

The ecumenical service at Dunblane Cathedral was a deeply moving tribute to the 16 children and their teacher killed on March 13, attended by a congregation of 600 and was by invitation only.

The Reverend Colin McIntosh, Minister at Dunblane Cathedral said: "The service was called 'Out of Darkness, Into Light',

I think it was an appropriate remembering of the children and their teacher and also a help to us all in the healing process".

Bad Year for Peace
Mood of depression justified

It has been a bad year for the peace process in Northern Ireland and there is scant chance of it getting much better.

If there is a mood of depression in Belfast this morning it is justified. The bombing of the Lisburn Army headquarters is the ultimate sign of frustration.

The peace process which began in optimism two years ago is bogged down in the petty feuds of Northern Ireland's tortured politics.

The IRA may try to establish a fresh ceasefire but, after the events of this year it is inconceivable that anyone would believe

them or be willing to admit Sinn Fein to talks without concrete expression of a willingness to uphold a ceasefire.

Republicans and Loyalists alike are becoming restless for action, whether it be round the negotiating table or on the streets.

Yet the Lisburn outrage, on the eve of the Tory Party conference, will only serve to strengthen Government resolve.

Glasgow and the South West
Dry with broken cloud and sunny intervals. Cloud increasing overnight may bring rain by dawn. Freshening SW wind.
Max 13 C (54 F), Min 8 C (46 F)

What a farce

There's only one word for yesterday's Scotland versus Estonia football farce ...ESTONISHING!

We turn up, play for three seconds and leave the park, clearly the victors by default, since they haven't even bothered to attend.

Now we've got to wait until November to find out the result.

Good job your coupon isn't depending on it!

Weather
24-hour Forecast

3

Question

Does the international aspect of the topic add to the study of the media? Could you carry out any kind of media comparison within your own country, for example rural/urban local news? Would this require contact with other schools or could it be run on the Internet without partners? In what way would the issues discussed differ from those in the described example?

Internet support for the topic

Making contact with other schools

Newsgroups:
news:k12.chat.teacher

Help with creating a newspaper on the Web

Creating Web pages:
http://web66.coled.umn.edu/Cookbook/contents.html

Newspapers published on the Internet

International newspaper sites

The two Uniform Resource Locators given below will
both link you to newspapers around the world. They do
not necessarily include the same newspapers.

http://www.uncg.edu:80/~cecarr/news/

This site allows you to select by continent and then by
country. It is a good site from which to choose a
newspaper to study as it gives guidance as to the type
of news covered, how current the news will be and
whether or not there is an English version. For example,
from this site you can go to a newspaper from the
Czech Republic which will not only be in English but is
also kept up to date:

http://www.coba.wright.edu/bie/paper.htm

The above site gives access to newspapers for every
state in the USA, plus links to other countries around
the world by clicking on the name of the state or
country.

Some useful sites for on-line newspapers in Britain

The Sunday Times
http://www.sunday-times.co.uk/

The Daily Telegraph
http://www.telegraph.co.uk/

The Times
http://www.the-times.co.uk/

The Scotsman
http://www.scotsman.com/index.html

The Herald
http://www.cims.co.uk/herald/

The Daily Record and Sunday Mail
http://www.record-mail.co.uk/rm/

For further help with your project we have included a worksheet and a table which can be found on pages 110 and 112.

Chapter 9
Space: An exploration project

Introduction

'**M**en who have worked together to reach the stars
are not likely to descend together into the
depths of war and desolation'
US Senator Lyndon Baines Johnson, 1958

Perhaps one of the most exciting events of the
twentieth century has been the exploration of space.
Man has orbited the earth, walked on the moon and
investigated the possibility of life on other planets and
in other universes.

The study of space is always an interesting project for
children to undertake, but using the Internet can lift the
project into another dimension! As a global resource
centre the Internet is immediate, as a means of global
communication it is an amazing method of contacting
people involved in space research, and as a global library
it allows access to a vast range of information that no
books could provide and can lead to links with schools
throughout the world. We have suggested a way to
conduct a space project in this chapter.

There is a wealth of information available on the Internet. Many space related sites are designed specifically for children and provide activities at an appropriate level. It is important however that the teacher views all sites in advance to decide if the content is suitable for the pupils.

Case Study: A space exploration project

Recent discoveries which suggest the possibility of life having existed on Mars could be an ideal starting point for your space project.

This will lead to a lesson on our own planet and what supports life on earth. Direct the pupils to sites on the Internet to gather information about the planets and moons in our solar system. Pupils can then produce reports on planets which they think could support life and give reasons for their choices.

They will also be able to print out amazing graphics from these sites. The information gathered can be used

to create a model of our solar system, a star map and be used as a stimulus for art work. There are sites dedicated totally to space art work and you may wish to allow your children to visit these.

Watching NASA

The children can keep a log book of all their space activities, and also those of NASA, for the duration of the project. This is one aspect of the project that is unique to the Internet. Children will have almost immediate access to the same information as the scientists at NASA! Some Internet resources can, if necessary, be printed and then used by pupils for off-computer work but, in order to fully experience the excitement of up-to-date information as presented on, for example, the NASA Today site, it is necessary to spend a significant amount of time on-line. This will raise awareness of the fact that there are daily developments which are not always covered in depth by the media. There is more to space research and development than the major missions which feature on the news.

Today at NASA:
http://www.hq.nasa.gov/office/pao/NewsRoom/today.html

When I grow up I want to be . . . an astronaut

This will lead to a discussion on how we travel in space and how people are chosen to be astronauts. Direct children to sites which contain details of astronaut selection procedures. The children can have fun creating their own programmes to prepare them for astronaut selection tests which have been designed by the class.

Once they have successfully passed their selection procedure they can contact astronauts from previous missions, by electronic mail, to learn of their experiences. Pupils will discover that while in space the astronauts carry out a number of scientific experiments.

Blast off!

Before your pupils are allowed to try out any 'experiments' they must first be launched into space, and this cannot happen until they have built a rocket. At the site for physical science teachers you will find extremely useful details on rocketry.

Debriefing

The children will now have completed their space exploration mission part of the project and it is now time for them to evaluate what they discovered. They will also investigate what was accomplished during actual missions by accessing Internet sites which detail former missions. A timeline of space could be created and displayed as a culmination of the project. (The children could even create a comic strip of their own mission and will find the AERO and SPACE COMIC site useful!)

You may decide to limit your pupils' investigations to certain decades, countries or types of missions. In fact there is such a wealth of information that any topic chosen could become a major project in its own right.

Further development

- It is possible to extend a space project beyond the confines of your classroom and to collaborate with others around the world. There are sites dedicated to collaborative projects.
- Information found about the planets could stimulate an interest in the galaxies and an astronomy project could be a spin off. There are many astronomical sites including those from the Observatories of Edinburgh and Cambridge.
- Such a project can also lead to a language project with children writing science fiction stories. Interesting if unbelievable information can be found at the UFO folklore site.

Question

Many suggestions are made in this example as to how the Internet can support the topic. What aspects of this topic could not be developed without access to the Internet? What other (non Internet) resources are available to your school? For your pupils, in your school, which activities would best be carried out on the Internet and which would be best supported by local, or school based resources?

Internet support for the topic

There is a wealth of sites on the World Wide Web dedicated to space and similar topics and there is not room in this chapter to detail all of them. The following Uniform Resource Locators are the most relevant sites for the space project described in the chapter. Some of them are duplicated under more than one heading and many of them also have links to other good sites.

Astronauts

Biographies of astronauts:
http://www.jsc.nasa.gov/Bios/htmlbios/

Apollo 11:
http://www.gsfc.nasa.gov/hqpao/apollo_11.html

Apollo 11 mission highlights:
http://www.ksc.gov/history/apollo/apollo-11/apollo-11html

How to become an astronaut:
http://www.ksc.nasa.gov/facts/faq12.html

Letters from astronauts:
http://titania.osf.hq.nasa.gov/Welcome.html

Information about astronauts:
http://128.165.1.1/solarsys/people.htm

SAREX – Shuttle Amateur Radio Experiment:
http://www.gsfc.nasa.gov/sarex/sarex_mainpage.html

Astronauts – A Student Project:
http://quest.arc.nasa.gov/smore/student/bears.html

Information about planets

Arizona Mars K-12 Education Program:
http://esther.la.asu.edu/asu_tes/TES_Editor/educ_activities_info.html

Life on Mars?:
http://www.jsc.nasa.gov/pao/flash/

Planetary fact sheets:
http://nssdc.gsfc.nasa.gov/planetary/planetfact.html

Stars and galaxies:
http://www.telescope.org/btl/data/starmenu.au

The Nine Planets:
http://www.norcol.ac.uk/nineplanets/

Weather

Athena/Tracking Space Weather:
http://inspire.ospi.wednet.edu:8001/curric/space/solterr/spacewx.html

Rocketry

Physical Science Teacher's Guide with activities:
http://www.lerc.nasa.gov/Other_Groups/K-12/TRC/Rockets/RocketActivitiesHome.html

Activities, quizzes and lesson plans

Auroras – Paintings in the sky:
http://netra.exploratorium.edu/learning_studio/auroras/

Mt Wilson Observatory Education:
http://www.mtwilson.edu/Education/

Kid's Space:
http://www.kids_space.org/

NASA/Goddard Space Flight Center:
http://www.gsfc.nasa.gov/education/education_home.html

STELLAR Activities:
http://stellar.arc.nasa.gov/index.html

Downloads and links to software programs

Astronomy Village: Investigating the Universe:
http://www.cotf.edu/AV/

ExInEd:
http://www.stsci.edu/exined_html/exined/

Space Telescope Electronic Information Service:
http://www.stsci.edu/

Graphics

A Photo Gallery of the Universe:
http://oposite.stsci.edu/pubinfo/Pictures.html

NASA Online Educational resources:
http://www.nasa.gov/nasa_online_education.html

Stars and galaxies:
http://www.telescope.org/btl/data/starmenu.au

StarMap:
http://www.mtwilson.edu/Services/StarMap/

Space Colouring Book:
http://tommy.jsc.nasa.gov/~woodfill/SPACEED/SEHHTML/color.html

Space Image libraries:
http://www.okstate.edu/aesp/image.html

Visual Media Collections:
**http://www.sils.umich.edu/~jweise/vmcb/html/corral/
Space_Scienc_Space_Resear.html**

The Messier Catalog:
http://seds.lpl.arizona.edu/messier/Messier.html

Views of the Solar System:
http://128.165.1.1/solarsys/

Welcome to the Planets:
ttp://pds.jpl.nasa.gov/planets/

JSC Imagery Services:
http://images.jsc.nasa.gov/

Movies and sound files

Apollo 11: **http://www.gsfc.nasa.gov/hqpao/apollo_11.html**

Space Movies cinema:
http://tommy.jsc.nasa.gov/~woodfill/SPACEED/SEHHTML/movies.html

History of space exploration

Mt Wilson Observatory education:
http://www.mtwilson.edu/Education/

Lunar exploration:
http://nssdc.gsfc.nasa.gov/planetary/lunar/apollo_25th.html

People:
http://128.165.1.1/solarsys/people.htm

History of space exploration:
http://nauts.com/histpace/histpace.html

Notable Manned & Unmanned Spacecraft:
http://nauts.com/histpace/vehiclepage.html

General information

BNSC – UK Space Activities 1995–1996:
http://www.open.gov.uk/bnsc/acts0.htm

Royal Greenwich Observatory Information Leaflets:
http://www.ast.cam.ac.uk/pubinfo/leaflets

Mount Wilson Institute:
http://www.mtwilson.edu/index.html

European Space Agency:
http://www.esrin.esa.it/htdocs/esa/esa.html

The Hubble Space Telescope:
http://www.stemnet.nf.ca/~cfowler/hubble.htm

Links

Astronomy and space:
http://www.npac.syr.edu/textbook/kidsweb/astronomy.html

British National Space Centre:
http://www.open.gov.uk/bnsc/main001.htm

Cambridge Astronomy:
http://www.ast.cam.ac.uk:80/

Canadian Space Guide:
http://www.space.ca/

Classroom of the Future:
http://www.cotf.edu/

Florida Today, Space Online:
http://www.flatoday.com/

Hotlist of Space Science Topics:
http://sln.fi.edu/tfi/hotlists/space.html

Liftoff to Space Exploration:
http://liftoff.msfc.nasa.gov/

NASA Kennedy Space Centre Home Page:
http://www.ksc.nasa.gov:80/

NASA Online Educational resources:
http://www.nasa.gov/nasa_online_education.html

Office of Space Flight:
http://titania.osf.hq.nasa.gov/Welcome.html

Royal Observatory Edinburgh:
http://www.roe.ac.uk/index.html

Space Explorer's Guide:
http://nyquist.ee.ualberta.ca/%7Ewanigar/spacelink/space_link.html

Athena: Space and Astronomy:
http://inspire.ospi.wednet.edu:8001/curric/space/index.html

Spacelink:
http://spacelink.msfc.nasa.gov/

Johnson Space Center:
http://www.jsc.nasa.gov/

The Hubble Space Telescope:
http://www.stemnet.nf.ca/~cfowler/hubble.htm

Glossary

Glossary of terms and people:
http://seds.lpl.arizona.edu/billa/tnp/help.html

Up-to-date sites

The NASA Homepage:
http://www.gsfc.nasa.gov/NASA_homepage.html

Space Calendar:
http://newproducts.jpl.nasa.gov:80/calendar/

S.P.A.C. – Space, Planetary and Astronomical Cyber-Experience:
http://www.nss.org/space/

Today at NASA:
http://www.hq.nasa.gov/office/pao/NewsRoom/today.html

NASA Television:
http://www.jsc.nasa.gov/pao/media/ntv.html

Links to other projects

Aerospace Education Services Program:
http://www.okstate.edu/aesp/AESP.html

Athena:
http://inspire.ospi.wednet.edu:8001/

Classroom of the Future:
http://www.cotf.edu/

Information Infrastructure Technology and Applications:
http://iita.ivv.nasa.gov/

Online Interactive Projects:
http://quest.arc.nasa.gov/interactive/index.html

Specific education programmes and links

Aerospace Education Services Program:
http://www.okstate.edu/aesp/AESP.html

Quest: NASA's K-12 Internet Initiative:
http://quest.arc.nasa.gov/

Sites specifically for teachers and children

Arizona Mars K-12 Education Program:
http://esther.la.asu.edu/asu_tes/TES_Editor/educ_activities_info.html

Astronomy and Space:
http://www.npac.syr.edu/textbook/kidsweb/astronomy.html

On-line space comics:
http://tommy.jsc.nasa.gov/~woodfill/SPACEED/SEHHTML/aspace1.html

K-12 Astronomy:
http://www.ceismc.gatech.edu/BusyT/astro.html

NASA LeRC Program:
http://www.lerc.nasa.gov/Other_Groups/K-12/K-12_homepage.html

Space: The Final Frontier:
http://alexia.lis.uiuc.edu/~watts/space.html

Space Educators' Handbook Homepage:
http://tommy.jsc.nasa.gov/~woodfill/SPACEED/SEHHTML/

StarChild:
http://heasarc.gsfc.nasa.gov/docs/StarChild/StarChild.html

Teacher's Resource Center:
http://quest.arc.nasa.gov/smore/teachers/index.html

Art

Chesley Bonestell Art Gallery:
http://www.secapl.com/bonestell/Top.html

Space Art HomePage:
http://tommy.jsc.nasa.gov/~woodfill/SPACEED/SEHHTML/spaceart.html

Astrology/UFOs/Science fiction

Science Fiction/Space Technology:
http://tommy.jsc.nasa.gov/~woodfill/SPACEED/SEHHTML/scifi.html

UFO Folklore:
http://www.qtm.net/geibdan/framemst.html

Space missions

Apollo 11: **http://www.gsfc.nasa.gov/hqpao/apollo_11.html**

Apollo 11 mission highlights:
http://www.ksc.nasa.gov/history/apollo/apollo-11/apollo-11.html

S/MORE – Shuttle-MIR:
http://quest.arc.nasa.gov/smore/index.html

Shuttle Launch Countdown HomePage:
http://www.ksc.nasa.gov/shuttle/countdown/

The space Shuttle:
http://seds.lpl.arizona.edu/ssa/index2.html

The NASA Shuttle Web Archives:
http://shuttle.nasa.gov/index.html/

Space Station Mir:
http://www.osf.hq.nasa.gov/mir/Welcome.html

**For further help with your project we have
included two worksheets which can be found on
pages 113 and 114.**

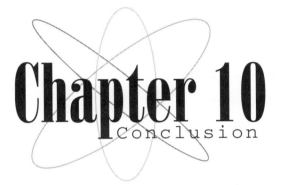

Chapter 10
conclusion

This book sets out to describe how the Internet can support learning and teaching. It was not intended to teach you how to use particular programs, or to describe the mechanics of connecting to the Internet in the first place (although you may have picked up some of this along the way).

Early chapters introduced and tried to demystify the Internet. Broad methods of using the Internet in the context of learning and teaching were introduced. Some simple practical issues were dealt with. Also some suggestions were made about where to find further information. These chapters were primarily intended to prepare you with some degree of confidence. Chapters 5 to 9, detail particular examples of educational uses.

We do not believe in using the Internet just because it is there. You should always examine the curricular aims of an activity and ensure that any activity you plan is relevant and meets your aims in a cost-effective manner. As far as possible we gave practical examples which hopefully gave a good idea of the value of the suggested activities.

We are not suggesting however that these are the only activities which will benefit from access to the Internet, or even that they are the best examples. In fact we would be very pleased to hear of any better ideas that you devise yourself, or other projects in which you find yourself involved. We hope that our suggestions inspire you with the confidence to experiment and that the examples, though not meeting your precise needs, give you ideas which you can take up and adapt to your own situation.

This book tried to answer some of the questions which you may have about the Internet and its educational value, but just as important are the questions it asked you. We hope that by asking you to analyse what we suggested, and by supporting you as you consider the answers, we can help you to arrive at a better understanding of the value of the Internet for you in your own situation.

Please feel free to get in touch with us and let us know how you are progressing as you take your schools into Cyberspace!

Morag F. Cunningham:
m.f.cunningham@strath.ac.uk

Fionna H. Kent:
f.h.kent@strath.ac.uk

David Muir:
d.d.muir@strath.ac.uk

Sports in Cyberspace

Worksheet 1 (see Chapter 5)

The Cyberspace Odyssey of Jason and the Cybernauts

You are the Cybernauts on an expedition to Ancient Greece

When you start your journey you find that blocking your way are enormous creatures each with only one eye. They will not allow you to continue. These creatures are protected by one of the gods.

Go to:

http://www.intergate.net/uhtml/.jhunt/greek_myth/greek_myth.html

Which god must you persuade to tell the creatures to let you pass?

_____

_____

_____

Print the story of how the creatures and this god became friends.

The god agrees to help if you bring back a dog with more than one head. Where does this dog live and what does it do? (Hint the links from the site above will help!)

_____

_____

_____

Print a picture of this dog.

The god tells the creature to let you pass but beware you are not yet safe. The god gives you a warning. As a result of this you decide to listen to your personal stereos as you sail across the water. Why?

_____

_____

_____

This page is photocopiable
© Cunningham, Kent and Muir, published by Hodder and Stoughton Educational 1997

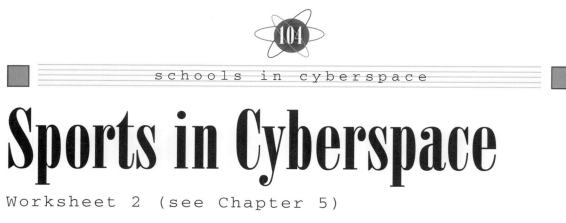
Sports in Cyberspace

Worksheet 2 (see Chapter 5)

To answer the questions on this worksheet you will have to use links to take you to different pages.

Go to:

http://www.venus.net/~nwashel2/olympic.games.html

There is a motto for the Modern Olympic Games. Write this in English and also in Latin.

_____

_____

_____

Who wrote this and what nationality was he

_____

_____

_____

The Olympics began in Ancient Greece. How were winners rewarded then? In what way is that different from what happens now?
In the boxes opposite draw a picture of an awards ceremony in Ancient Greece and one in a Modern Games.

_____

_____

_____

The Vikings

Worksheet 1 (see Chapter 6)

Speak like a Viking

You will need a tape recorder and a pencil

Go to:

http://odin.nls.no/viking/e/heritage/evoices.htm

In the table below write how the Vikings would say each of the phrases.

I am a Viking from Iceland	
One, two, three, four	
Greetings from Iceland	
Good night	
Iceland is an island	
The Vikings travelled a lot	

Now click on a sound file and listen very carefully.

Tape record each other saying the same words. You can check if you have done it well by listening again to Gisli.

Tape record each other saying each of the phrases in the language of the Vikings.

Give a reason why the people in Britain and the Vikings who sailed there could understand each other.

_____

_____

_____

_____

_____

_____

When you bring this worksheet to be checked by the teacher you will be asked who you are. Be ready to answer in the language of the Vikings 'I am a Viking from Iceland'.

_____

_____

_____

The Vikings

Worksheet 2 (see Chapter 6)

King Bluetooth and Palnatroke

Go to:

http://odin.nls.no/viking/e/life/sports/earchery.htm

Follow the links to find the story of King Bluetooth and Palnatroke who thought he was a good archer.

In the boxes below draw pictures to tell the story.

There is a story about a man, who was not a Viking, called William Tell. Find this story in the library.

What did you find out about the two stories?

_____

_____

_____

Where did William Tell live?

_____

_____

_____

Which story happened first?

_____

_____

_____

The Aztecs

Worksheet 1 (see Chapter 7)

Aztec Calendars

Go to:

http://www.ironhorse.com/~nagual/alma.html

Under the picture you will see today's date in the Julian Calendar.

Which event does the picture depict?

_____

Name the morning stars. (Hint – the graphics are links!)

_____

_____

Write today's date using the Aztec glyphs.

Can you find today's date in Spanish? Write it down.

_____

_____

_____

Note down three interesting events that happened on this day in history.

_____

_____

_____

_____

This page is photocopiable

The Aztecs

Worksheet 2 (see Chapter 7)

Sunstones and Picnics

Go to:

http://www.public.iastate.edu/~rjsalvad/scmfaq/calendar.html

Look carefully at the sunstone. Who was the artist?

_____

_____

_____

Which month means Flamingo in Nahuatl?

_____

_____

_____

There is a link on this page to the 'Little Feast of the Dead'. Follow this link
and write below what happens on this day.

_____

_____

_____

_____

_____

_____

_____

© Cunningham, Kent and Muir, published by Hodder and Stoughton Educational 1997

Write down one of the Mexican dishes that might be prepared for a picnic on that day.

_____

_____

_____

In the box below draw a picture of what you think the dish will look like.

Newspaper Project 1

Group Planning Activity (see Chapter 8)

Study the selection of current newspapers and compare:

1 The newspaper vocabulary e.g. by-lines, photo captions, jump lines etc. These are present in all papers but often missed in school newspapers. *Refer to the example provided.*

2 Look at the design of the front pages and discuss the type face used for:
a the masthead
b headlines
c main body of text

3 Study the use made of fonts.
a sans serif or serif fonts
b number of different fonts (*lots/few*)

4 Look at the front page and decide which parts of the page catch the eye and in what order.

Is it the headline?

Is it the photograph?

Is it an advert?

Where on the page is the headline?

How large are the headlines, sub headlines?

Is the photograph just above the midpoint?

Is it a large photograph? (*shouldn't be too small*)

Are the pictures square or oblong? (*can be cropped or trimmed*)

5 Adverts and articles.

a Where are the adverts on the page?

b How many stories are on the page?

6 Other details to study and discuss.

How many columns? Note the gap between columns.

Any dividing lines or borders for pictures and adverts?

Approximate number of words per line? (*short lines in long columns make difficult reading*)

Effective use of white space? (*don't just try to fill the gaps*)

Layout of the pages in columns or blocks. (*a block may cross more than one column*)

Newspapers Project Information (see Chapter 8)

Benefits of a newspaper project

Skills	Knowledge	Attitudes
Decision making	Newspaper terms and personnel	Respect views of others
Organisation	Caption effectiveness	Developing an interest in current affairs
Information Technology	Current Affairs	Awareness of the global community
Selection process	Effective forms of communication	Objectivity
Editing	Genre of newspapers – Tabloid/Broadsheet	Discretion
Delegation	Political bias	Co-operation
Genre/Style of writing	Audience awareness	Consideration
Planning	Role of newspapers	Collaboration
Time management	English language	
Presentation and layout		
Research		
Communication		
Dealing with pressure		

© Cunningham, Kent and Muir, published by Hodder and Stoughton Educational 1997

Space

Worksheet 1 (see Chapter 9)

How to be an astronaut

The space ship is almost ready. All that is needed now is a crew. It is your chance to be chosen as one of the astronauts. How will you do this?

Go to:

http://www.ksc.nasa.gov/facts/faq12.html

If you want to be a NASA astronaut of which country MUST you be a citizen?

_____

What should your blood pressure be and what is the minimum height for the basic qualification?

_____

Where should you write to obtain the application package?

_____

Now to find out more about what it is like to be on a mission.

Go to:

http://www.gsfc.nasa.gov/hqpao/apollo_11.html

Follow the graphic link to Mission Info and then on to Mission Overview. Who were the crew?

_____

Go back to the main menu. Now follow the link to the Images and find out what Astronaut Buzz Aldrin has on his head.

_____

Space

Worksheet 2 (see Chapter 9)

Space reports

You have to write a report about each of the plants in our Solar System. This worksheet will help you gather information.

Go to:

http://www.norcol.ac.uk/nineplanets/

Begin with our own planet. Follow the link to that!

What is Earth's position in relation to the Sun and how far would you need to travel to reach the sun?

_____

Now go back to the previous site. By following the links to the nine planets can you find out the answers to these questions?

Which is the third largest planet?

_____

Which planet is more than twice as massive as all the other planets?

_____

Which planet is the farthest from the Sun?

_____

What is the name of the music to which you can listen?

_____

Draw the symbol for each planet beside its name.

_____

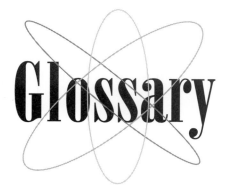

Glossary

Cyberspeak Translator

This glossary is not comprehensive. It tries to pick out the main terms used in this book and some of the terms in more common use. In particular it will show many of the commonly used acronyms and give the expanded version as well as an explanation.

It may not surprise you to learn that there are explanations of common terms available on the Internet. One of the best can be found at the Free On-line Dictionary Of Computing Terms:

http://wombat.doc.ic.ac.uk/foldoc/

This dictionary is perhaps too technical in places for some people, but it is incredibly comprehensive and is updated at regular intervals. (It does lighten the technical descriptions with a small dose of humour. See for example the definition of 'off-line world' and the 'see also' links on the 'infinite loop' definition.)

Acceptable Use Policy: A set of rules which determine the use to which a system may be put. Typically this states the responsibilities of pupils, parents and teachers, as well as the penalties for inappropriate uses.

AUP: See *Acceptable Use Policy*

Bookmarks: A store of *links* which allow a person to quickly locate documents to which you wish to refer frequently.

Browser: A program which allows a person to read *World Wide Web* documents.

Cyberspace: A term invented by science fiction writer William Gibson. It is a notional 'information-space' which people can move through accessing the information. (If you think this definition is unhelpful, William Gibson described it as 'the there that isn't there'!)

E-mail: See *Electronic mail*

Electronic mail: A system which passes messages automatically from one computer to another.

FAQ: See *Frequently Asked Questions*

Favourites: Another name for *Bookmarks*

Frequently Asked Questions: The main purpose of a Frequently Asked Questions document is to provide answers to commonly asked questions on a given topic.

HTML: See *Hypertext Markup Language*

HTTP: See *Hypertext Transfer Protocol*

Hypermedia: Cross-referenced *links* which allow the reader to move easily from one document to another. The *link* can be indicated by a piece of text, a graphic, a movie or any other object which can be displayed on a computer screen. Often a pointing device such as a mouse is used to click on the hypermedia object.

Hypertext: Cross-referenced *links* which allow the reader to move easily from one document to another. Often a pointing device such as a mouse is used to click on the hypertext. Hypertext is just one example of a *hypermedia* object.

Hypertext Markup Language: This is a language which describes the format of *World Wide Web* page using markup tags.

Hypertext Transfer Protocol: An access method identifier, in other words it shows what type of information is accessed by this locator. In it means that the information which will be accessed is a *World Wide Web* page.

Internet: A *network* of networks. Many networks around the world are linked to each other. This means that when you attach a computer to the Internet, it is possible to access information held on millions of computers spread around the world.

Internet Service Provider: This is a company which offers other companies or individuals access to the *Internet*.

ISP: See *Internet Service Provider.*

Link: A reference from one point in a document to another. See also *hypertext*.

Mailing list: A single *electronic mail* address which in fact is connected to many other addresses. Sending a message to a mailing list will cause it to be copied to everyone else who subscribes to the list.

Network: A network is simply a group of computers which are linked together so that they can share information.

Newsgroups: A collection of topic groups. Messages are sent to a topic group and anyone who wishes to can read and comment on the messages.

Search engine: A program which searches the *Internet* for information and catalogues what it finds. People can then search the catalogue for *links* to specific information.

Uniform Resource Locator: A standard for specifying the location of an object on the *Internet*. Extensively used on the *World Wide Web*.

URL: See *Uniform Resource Locator*

World Wide Web: An information retrieval system which makes extensive use of *hypertext* to link related sources of information.

WWW: See *World Wide Web*

Index